HOW COMPUTER GRAPHICS WORK

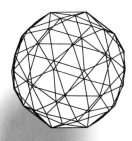 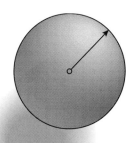 

HOW COMPUTER GRAPHICS WORK

JEFF PROSISE

Illustrated by
GARY SUEN

Ziff-Davis Press
Emeryville, California

Development Editor	Kim Haglund
Copy Editor	Kelly Green
Technical Reviewer	Neil J. Rubenking
Project Coordinator	Cort Day
Proofreader	Carol Burbo
Cover Illustration	Regan Honda, Gary Suen
Cover Design	Carrie English
Book Design	Carrie English
Screen Graphics Editor	Dan Brodnitz
Illustrator	Gary Suen
Word Processing	Howard Blechman
Page Layout	M.D. Barrera
Indexer	Anne Leach

Ziff-Davis Press books are produced on a Macintosh computer system with the following applications: FrameMaker®, Microsoft® Word, QuarkXPress®, Adobe Illustrator®, Adobe Photoshop®, Adobe Streamline™, MacLink®*Plus*, Aldus® FreeHand™, Collage Plus™.

If you have comments or questions or would like to receive a free catalog, call or write:
Ziff-Davis Press
5903 Christie Avenue
Emeryville, CA 94608
1-800-688-0448

ISBN 1-56276-242-7

Manufactured in the United States of America
♻ This book is printed on paper that contains 50% total recycled fiber of which 20% is de-inked postconsumer fiber.
10 9 8 7 6 5 4 3 2 1

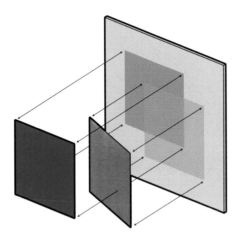

Dedicated to the memory of my good friend and colleague, Dale Lewallen. May his spirit live on forever.

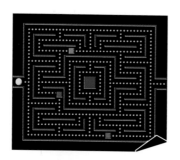
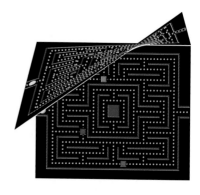

Introduction x

PART 1

Computer Graphics in Today's World
1

Chapter 1
Flight Simulators 4

Chapter 2
Computer-Aided Design 10

Chapter 3
Medical Imaging 16

Chapter 4
Video Games 24

PART 2

Computer Graphics Fundamentals
31

Chapter 5
Computers, Pixels,
and Color 34

Chapter 6
Palettes and Palette
Optimization 44

Chapter 7
Drawing, Filling, and Scan
Converting 50

Chapter 8
Texts and Fonts 60

Chapter 9
Antialiasing 68

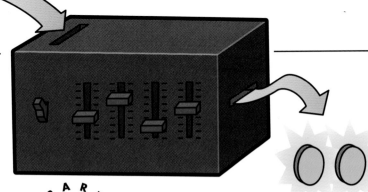

PART 3

Images and Image Processing
73

Chapter 10
Getting Images into the Computer 76

Chapter 11
Bitmapped File Storage.........84

Chapter 12
Image Compression 90

Chapter 13
Image Enhancement and Special Effects 98

PART 4

Three-Dimensional Modeling and Rendering
107

Chapter 14
Representing Objects in Three-Dimensional Space ...110

Chapter 15
Viewing Objects in Three-Dimensional Space: Projections.............................114

Chapter 16
Shading, Lighting, and Surface Removal..................................118

Chapter 17
Ray Tracing 128

Chapter 18
Solid Modeling...............134

PART 5

Final Frontiers
141

Computer Animation 144

Chapter 20
Fractals 152

Chapter 21
Morphing 162

Chapter 22
Virtual Reality 168

Index......................................175

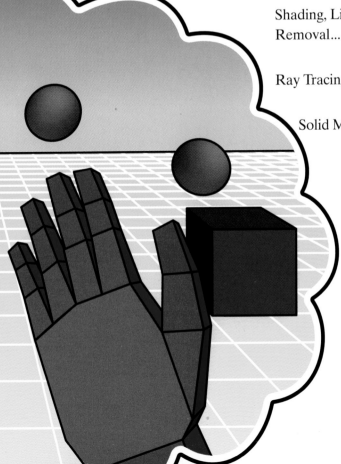
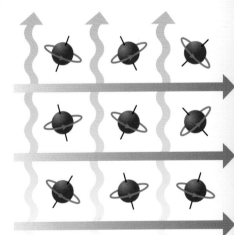

A book such as this one is not the work of one person, but of many. I'd like to take a moment to thank all the members of the production team who helped turn my manuscript and sketches into the final product that you hold in your hands. In particular, I wish to thank Gary Suen, who is responsible for the book's beautiful illustrations; Kim Haglund, who, in the role of developmental editor, served as point person for the writing, editing, and illustrating and made sure all the pieces fit together; Cort Day and Kelly Green, who ably filled the roles of project coordinator and copy editor, respectively; Neil Rubenking, whose technical acumen and talent for explaining complex subjects in understandable terms never ceases to amaze me; and Cindy Hudson, who afforded me the opportunity to write this book.

Special thanks are owed to several people in the computer industry who provided technical background to increase my understanding of computer graphics and helped me acquire the sample images that I couldn't generate myself. Albert Yan of Apple Computer was especially helpful in describing to me how digital cameras work. Sara Wilson and Bob Gann of Hewlett-Packard provided a wealth of information about color scanners. Brita Womack and Brian Massey of Vibrant Graphics and Beth Parkinson of Autodesk were instrumental in helping me demonstrate antialiasing. Terry McArdle of Eastman Kodak was gracious enough to allow me to use the parrot image from the Kodak Photo Sampler to demonstrate the fundamentals of image display and processing. Finally, a heartfelt thanks to the folks at GE Medical Systems, who shared with me valuable technical literature describing the principles behind magnetic resonance imaging.

Computer graphics: For some, the term strikes up images of bar charts, colorful fractal whorls, and video games. For others, it invokes images of frighteningly long mathematical equations and complex computer algorithms. Neither perception is entirely correct, but neither is entirely incorrect, either. The truth lies somewhere in between.

My introduction to computer graphics came in 1983, when I bought my first personal computer—a Commodore 64—with the intention of writing some simple game programs. Imagine my surprise when I got home and learned that although the C64 had outstanding graphics capabilities (for that day and time, anyway), its built-in BASIC programming language lacked even rudimentary support for graphical operations. There was no LINE command, for example. Nor was there a command to switch the screen to graphics mode. My first attempt at graphics programming was a BASIC program that cleared the screen, pixel by pixel, using PEEKs and POKEs. That program took almost a minute and a half to run. Imagine that! You could literally *see* the pixels changing to black row by row, column by column. Clearly there had to be a better way. To write my game programs, I eventually had to learn assembly language (a very slow way to write very fast programs) and write my own screen-clearing and line-drawing routines, among others. It was painful at the time, but the experience gave me a firsthand knowledge of computer graphics that I couldn't have gotten in any other way.

You don't have to be a math whiz or a computer programmer to understand how computer graphics work. The goal of this book is to expose the principles behind modern computer graphics without straying into the arcane languages of math and computer science. In the acknowledgments to his 1988 bestseller *A Brief History of Time*, Stephen Hawking wrote of a colleague's warning that every equation he included in the book would halve the sales. He therefore elected to banish all equations with the exception of Einstein's famous $E=mc^2$. I decided to adopt the same philosophy for *How Computer Graphics Work*. You won't find any equations in this book. What you will find are colorful illustrations accompanied by clear, step-by-step explanations that describe how computers do what they do when they draw pictures.

As you read *How Computer Graphics Work*, you'll learn how bits and bytes in computer memory translate to colorful images on the computer screen, and how computers use clever tricks to line up those bits and bytes to form basic shapes such as lines, circles, and squares. At a higher level, you'll learn how morphing works (remember the famous liquid-metal man scenes in the movie *Terminator 2*?) and how a flight simulator draws three-dimensional images depicting the world outside the cockpit. You'll also learn how video games work, how images are digitally enhanced, how fractal images are created, how large graphics files are compressed to a fraction of their normal size, how scanners and digital cameras work, and much, much more.

A key tenet of this book is that computer graphics should be fun. And learning about them should be fun also. But this book wouldn't exist if not for the fact that computer graphics have practical and serious applications in the real world. Without computer graphics, we wouldn't have flight simulators, computer-aided design systems, MRI machines, and other marvels of modern science. If you haven't been exposed to these technologies directly, chances are you've been affected by them indirectly. The car you drive was probably designed on a computer. Commercial aircraft are piloted by men and women who, in addition to having logged thousands of hours of flight time, have trained extensively in flight simulators. In the 30-odd years in which they have been with us, computer graphics have become pervasive in our everyday lives. As computers become more ubiquitous, so too will computer graphics. The time to get acquainted with them is now.

COMPUTER GRAPHICS IN TODAY'S WORLD

CONTENTS

Chapter 1: Flight Simulators
4

Chapter 2: Computer-Aided Design
10

Chapter 3: Medical Imaging
16

Chapter 4: Video Games
24

OVERVIEW

A LOGICAL PLACE TO begin any discussion of computer graphics is with the question: What are computer graphics? Simply defined, computer graphics are images created by a computer. In the field of computer graphics, art imitates life; today's computers are capable of generating lifelike images that are virtually indistinguishable from the images captured in photographs. *Fractal images*—computer-generated pictures possessing infinite complexity—allow computers to simulate objects in nature, from plants to mountain ranges, while ray-tracing techniques enable computers to render pictures with realistic lighting effects. Computer graphics are not constrained by the boundaries of realism; sometimes they go far into the realm of the imaginary, as demonstrated by the computerized special effects you see in the movies.

The science of computer graphics began in the early 1960s when Ivan Sutherland, cofounder of the pioneering computer graphics firm of Evans & Sutherland, developed a sketching program for a TX-2 computer while pursuing his doctorate at MIT. Profuse research in the years since has advanced computer graphics to the current state of the art. Computer graphics no longer exist only in the halls of academia; they're everywhere, touching our lives in ways too numerous to count. They are used in the defense industry to bring out hard-to-see details in satellite photographs; in the manufacturing industry to design consumer products from hair dryers to aircraft; in engineering to visualize stresses and temperatures; in medicine to explore the inside of the human body; and in genetic research to draw pictorial models of helical strands of DNA. The list could go on and on.

In Part 1, we examine four modern-day applications for computer graphics: flight simulators, computer-aided design, medical imaging, and video games. Each involves computer graphics in a very important way. None, in fact, would be feasible *without* computer graphics. Chapters 1 through 4 present overviews of these technologies and the roles that computer graphics play in them. Subsequent chapters will explore many aspects of the graphics that you'll see here in more detail, showing, for example, how a flight simulator's images are created.

Flight Simulators

CLOSE YOUR EYES for a moment and imagine that you're an airline pilot making an instrument approach through rain and low-hanging clouds to a fog-shrouded runway. A moderate crosswind applies pressure to your tail, like an unseen hand pressing sideways against the rear of the plane. You compensate by keeping your left foot pressed firmly against the rudder pedal. The rain pounds harder against the windshield as you approach ground level, and the single wiper blade on your side of the cockpit can barely keep up with the water impacting the plane's exterior and running backward along the fuselage in the boundary layer of air clinging to the plane's skin. No matter; your eyes are locked on your instruments while your copilot gazes out the windshield, searching for the lower limit of the ceiling that obscures the ground.

Suddenly, less than 800 feet from the ground, the plane's left engine loses 80 percent of its power. The aircraft spins wildly to the left under the yaw created by the right engine. At the same time, the wind shifts so that it's coming directly from behind, reducing the plane's air speed and robbing it of much-needed lift. The aircraft noses downward. You pull back on the yoke, at the same time slamming the right rudder pedal hard to the floor to counteract the movement produced by the nonmatching thrust. Your mind flashes back to air combat school, when you executed similar maneuvers with plenty of altitude in light, highly-maneuverable fighter craft. Right now you're only a few hundred feet from the ground, in a lumbering passenger jet with 120 people aboard. As you struggle to right the plane, the cockpit's ground proximity alarm sounds a shrill note and you catch your first glimpse of the runway lights—a quarter mile farther away than you thought and too high on the horizon to accommodate a conventional approach.

If this were reality, you—and your passengers and crew—would be in big trouble. But since it's only a simulation, you'll live to fly another day. Today's airline pilots train for a variety of adverse situations in sophisticated ground-based flight simulators, preparing for similar conditions should they ever occur in flight. Flight simulators do more than make air travel safer; they make it cheaper, too, by reducing the cost of pilot training.

Flight simulators are computer-generated virtual reality at its best. In a commercial flight simulator, the pilot sits enclosed in a detailed mock-up of the plane's cockpit. The windshield is actually a computer screen, driven by a high-speed computer that produces realistic images of the scenery outside the aircraft. Actuating cylinders outside the cockpit—also driven by computer—simulate the motion of flight by reproducing the roll, pitch, and yaw of the aircraft. The combination of sensory feedbacks imparts a sense of hurtling through space. Today's flight simulators are so realistic that a pilot can become proficient in flying a new plane without ever leaving the ground. Even inexpensive PC-based simulators provide a simulation of the flight experience that is sufficiently realistic for some purposes; many flight schools now use them to introduce new pilots to basic instruments, navigational skills, and other aspects of flight.

Flight simulators have always stood at the vanguard of real-time three-dimensional computer graphics. The better the graphics, the better the simulation. This chapter provides an inside look at how flight simulators work, and at the essential role that computer graphics play in the process. Later, in Part 4, you'll learn more about how three-dimensional computer graphics are produced, and how they are portrayed on a two-dimensional screen.

How Flight Simulators Work

4 Objects such as buildings, mountains, and runways are defined with simple geometric surfaces such as squares and rectangles. A control tower, for example, might consist of four long, vertical rectangles capped with a square. Hidden-surface algorithms ensure that surfaces that lie behind other surfaces—for instance, the rectangles forming the back of the tower—are not displayed.

3 Several times each second, the flight simulator's computer uses the geographical information stored in its database, combined with information about the aircraft's flight path and orientation, to generate a new view outside the cockpit. Because the screen is updated each time a new image is formed in computer memory, the scenery appears to fly by underneath. The more rapidly the computer can redraw the screen, the smoother and more realistic the aircraft's movement appears.

2 As the pilot "flies" the simulator with the cockpit controls, information is fed back to the computer. Raw data is transformed into meaningful flight information. If the yoke is turned to the left, the computer tilts the image on the pilot's screen to the right to create the illusion that the aircraft is banking toward the left. If the simulated cockpit is mounted on actuating cylinders, the right side of the cockpit is raised and the left side is lowered so the pilot will feel the banking motion.

1 The computer that drives the simulation process stores a database of information about the "world" outside the plane—terrain, buildings, wind speed and direction, and so on. This information is downloaded to the computer before the simulation starts so that the same simulator can be used to fly anywhere, and under any set of conditions. Graphical images produced by the computer are output to the screen that serves as the pilot's windshield. Input comes from the airplane controls inside the cockpit.

5 The use of *perspective*—the illusion that parallel lines drawn in space converge toward a vanishing point—lends realism to the scene. In reality, the two lines defining the runway borders run perfectly parallel. But to an observer within the scene, they appear to follow intersecting paths. Other computer-generated visual cues, such as a sky that fades from dark blue to light blue, enhance the effect.

6 In modern aircraft (and by extension in the simulators patterned after them), many of the cockpit instruments are not instruments at all, but small screens displaying images that look like instruments. These images are also computer-generated. The instrument computer may be part of the flight simulator's main computer, or it may be housed in a separate processing unit set up to serve the interior of the cockpit apart from the screen. Either way, these images are synchronized with the flight controls and imagery outside the cockpit to present a complete picture to the person piloting the simulator.

CHAPTER 2

Computer-Aided Design

FEW, IF ANY, applications for computer graphics have impacted an industry like computer-aided design (CAD) has impacted the fields of engineering and manufacturing. Before CAD was invented, engineering design drawings—precision line drawings illustrating how a product would look, with dimensions specifying the sizes and locations of individual features—were created by hand using pencils, T-squares, templates, and other mechanical drawing tools. Drawings were time-consuming to produce, and equally time-consuming to modify.

CAD changed the way designers worked by replacing drawing boards with graphics terminals and drawing tools with software commands. Instead of drawing a line with a pencil and a ruler, a CAD operator (the person using the CAD software) picks out two points on the screen, and the computer connects them with a line. Instead of creating a circle by tracing a circular cutout in a template, the operator specifies a center point and a radius, and the CAD software draws a circle. CAD drawings are generally easier to create than conventional pencil-on-paper drawings because recurring elements, such as the teeth on the perimeter of a gear, can be drawn once and then replicated as many times as necessary by the computer. Changes are also easier to make, because simple gestures such as pointing and clicking can erase an entire section of a drawing or reshape it to fit the designer's specifications.

CAD software has come a long way since it first came into use in the 1970s. A typical CAD system from that era consisted of a mainframe computer and several graphics terminals. Today, CAD software is available for all types of computers, from powerful mainframes to desktop PCs. It is still used to create design drawings, but its uses go far beyond that. Some CAD systems, for example, generate photographlike images enabling engineers to visualize what a part will look like before it is manufactured, and architects to see how a finished building will look before the first brick is even laid. Some CAD systems will create programs that drive computerized manufacturing machines (which in turn create the objects you see on the CAD screen), doing in a few seconds what once required programmers hours to do manually. And some perform common engineering calculations that were formerly done by hand.

The following illustration describes the process a designer might go through to model a simple object on the computer screen, giving you a general picture of how a CAD system works. Later, in Parts 2 and 4, you'll learn more about the techniques involved in displaying CAD images, including how the CAD software draws lines on the screen and how it removes hidden lines to produce a more realistic image.

How Computer-Aided Design Works

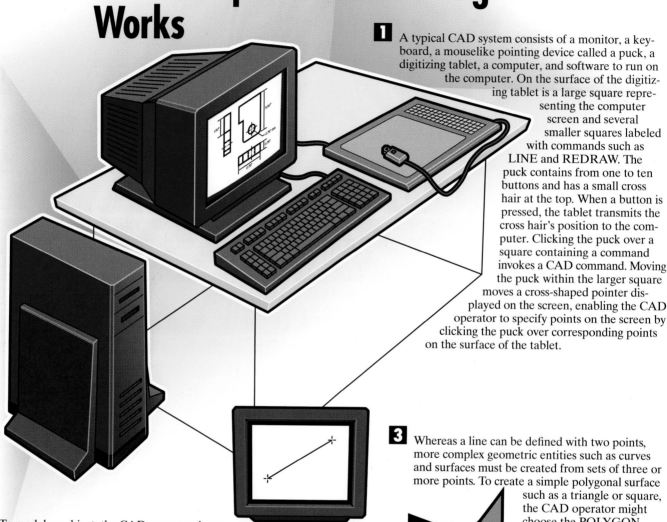

1 A typical CAD system consists of a monitor, a keyboard, a mouselike pointing device called a puck, a digitizing tablet, a computer, and software to run on the computer. On the surface of the digitizing tablet is a large square representing the computer screen and several smaller squares labeled with commands such as LINE and REDRAW. The puck contains from one to ten buttons and has a small cross hair at the top. When a button is pressed, the tablet transmits the cross hair's position to the computer. Clicking the puck over a square containing a command invokes a CAD command. Moving the puck within the larger square moves a cross-shaped pointer displayed on the screen, enabling the CAD operator to specify points on the screen by clicking the puck over corresponding points on the surface of the tablet.

2 To model an object, the CAD operator draws, one by one, the individual lines, circles, and other shapes (called entities) that make up the object. To draw a line, the operater clicks the square labeled LINE. He then moves the puck into the area of the digitizing tablet that corresponds to the screen and clicks once at each of the endpoints of the line; the CAD software then draws the line between them. As an alternative, the CAD operator may choose to enter the points' coordinates directly by typing them on the keyboard. The keyboard input option is particularly important on three-dimensional CAD systems, because the digitizing tablet is inherently a two-dimensional input device. Most CAD systems offer the operator a wide variety of input options for any given operation.

3 Whereas a line can be defined with two points, more complex geometric entities such as curves and surfaces must be created from sets of three or more points. To create a simple polygonal surface such as a triangle or square, the CAD operator might choose the POLYGON command and enter the coordinates of the surface's vertices. Curved surfaces can be approximated with many small polygons. On some CAD systems, curved surfaces can be modeled precisely by entering points along one of the curved edges.

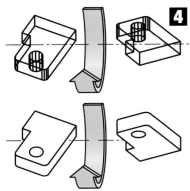

4 Once all the geometric entities are created, the CAD operator has a complete wire-frame model of the object. The model can be rotated about the x, y, and z axes to achieve the desired viewing angle. If the model contains surfaces, the CAD operator can ask the CAD software to remove hidden lines from the picture. Depending on the complexity of the object and the speed of the computer, this process can take from a few seconds to several minutes, because the CAD software must perform time-consuming computations on each surface to determine which parts of which surfaces are obscured by other surfaces.

5 If the CAD software supports shading and lighting, the CAD operator can also ask the computer to *render* the object—to display it as it will appear in real life. In preparation for this process, the CAD operator assigns each surface in the model a color and positions light sources throughout the scene. The CAD software uses the coloring and lighting information to compute a shade of color for every dot on the computer screen that corresponds to a visible surface, taking into account factors such as the angle and amount of light incident on the surface and the degree to which the surface reflects the light that hits it.

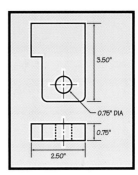

6 In order to create a conventional manufacturing drawing for the part, the CAD operator picks orthogonal views (views looking along the x, y, or z axis) from the model, pastes them into a new drawing, and adds dimensions specifying the size and location of individual features. To dimension a line, the CAD operator points to the ends of the line, and the software creates the dimension. On most modern CAD systems, dimensions are *associative*, meaning that they are tied to specific features of a part. An associative dimension changes if the feature that it is associated with it changes. If a circle's diameter changes, for example, the CAD software automatically updates the dimension specifying the circle's diameter.

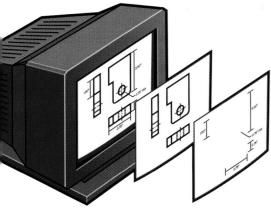

7 Most CAD systems support the concept of *layering*, which divides a drawing into discrete units, called layers, that can be turned on and off individually. A CAD operator might place lines and curves on one layer and dimensions on another. Then, to display geometry only, the operator could hide the dimensions by turning off the dimension layer.

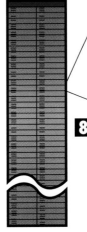

ENTITY DATABASE

TYPE	LINE (7)
X1	1
Y1	1
Z1	3
X2	10
Y2	6
Z2	-4

8 For each entity in the drawing, the CAD software stores a database entry that describes the entity. The entry for a line, for example, might contain seven numbers: one identifying the entity type (line), three specifying the x, y, and z coordinates of the line's first endpoint, and three specifying the x, y, and z coordinates of the other endpoint. (To include other line attributes such as line color and line type, the entry's definition could be expanded to hold additional values.) To redraw the image, the CAD software reads through the database of entries from top to bottom and draws each entity in turn on the screen.

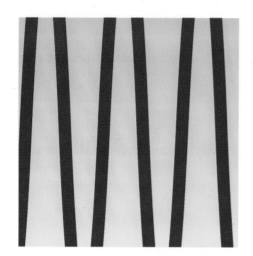

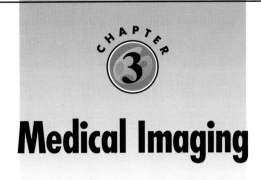

Medical Imaging

UNTIL A FEW short years ago, the only means physicians had to peer inside the human body was X-rays. Emerging medical technologies using computer graphics are rapidly changing that. Today, physicians can choose from a variety of computer-assisted medical imaging techniques for producing accurate, detailed pictures of the body's interior and of individual organs such as the heart, liver, and brain. Chief among these techniques are *computerized axial tomography*, better known as *CAT* (or simply *CT*), and *magnetic resonance imaging*, or *MRI*. Computer graphics play an important role in both.

CAT scans produce detailed images showing cross sections of the human body, similar to the view you have of the interior of an apple when you cut it down the middle. The word *tomography* comes from the Greek word *tomos*, meaning *section*. By controlling where the section is taken, a physician can zero in on a specific region of the body. Typically, the patient lies on his or her back on a table positioned perpendicular to a device called a *gantry,* which houses X-ray equipment. The patient is inserted through a circular opening in the gantry and positioned so that the area of the body that is the subject of the CAT scan rests within the opening. The gantry rotates about the patient and beams X-rays through the opening. The data from the X-rays is passed to a computer, which assembles a graphical representation of the information on a computer screen. If the physician needs additional information about surrounding tissues, several CAT scans can be taken a short distance apart to extend the analysis to three dimensions. CAT images are up to 100 times clearer than conventional x-ray images, and the total amount of radiation absorbed by the patient is about equal to the amount received from a standard chest x-ray.

MRI also produces detailed cross-sectional images of the body's interior, but without exposing the patient to X-rays or other forms of radiation. The patient is placed inside a large cylindrical magnet that generates a strong magnetic field. The magnetic field uniformly aligns the spin axes of atomic nuclei in the patient's body. The MRI machine then sends a pulse of radio-frequency (RF) energy through the body to upset the spin orientations of certain nuclei (typically the nuclei of hydrogen atoms, which are abundant in tissue). In this state, the unaligned nuclei resonate, producing weak RF signals that can be picked up by sensitive RF detectors. When the RF pulse dissipates,

RF detectors inside the MRI machine measure the rate of signal decay as the spinning nuclei return to their original orientations. This information is passed to a computer, which transforms the raw data into images detailing the interior of the human body. Different colors in the images reflect the differing atomic characteristics of the affected tissues, producing highly detailed—and colorful—cross sections of the body. Though the image is two-dimensional, slight and carefully applied variations in the magnetic field can lend MRI images a three-dimensional effect. In the future, supercomputers connected to three-dimensional displays will permit doctors to view MRI images in three dimensions.

In both CAT and MRI, the doctor sometimes introduces into the body a chemical dye solution known as a contrast agent to heighten visual contrast between adjoining tissues. This helps the computer distinguish between a particular organ or area of the body (for example, a bone joint) and the matter surrounding it, producing a better image. CAT and MRI find many applications in modern medicine, including the exploration of tumors, blood clots, and broken bones. Related imaging technologies such as *positron emission tomography* (*PET*), which draws pictures of activity within the brain, provide additional means for probing the interior of the human body.

Let's look more closely at how CAT and MRI work, and see how computer graphics fit into the picture.

How Computerized Axial Tomography Works

1 In preparation for a CAT scan, the patient is placed on a table and positioned so that the region of his or her body from which the image will be taken rests within the circular opening in the gantry. The top of the gantry houses an X-ray source and a *collimator* to arrange the X-rays into thin, parallel beams; the bottom contains X-ray detectors. In some cases, a physician will administer a chemical contrast agent prior to the scan to heighten visual contrast between the target area and surrounding tissues.

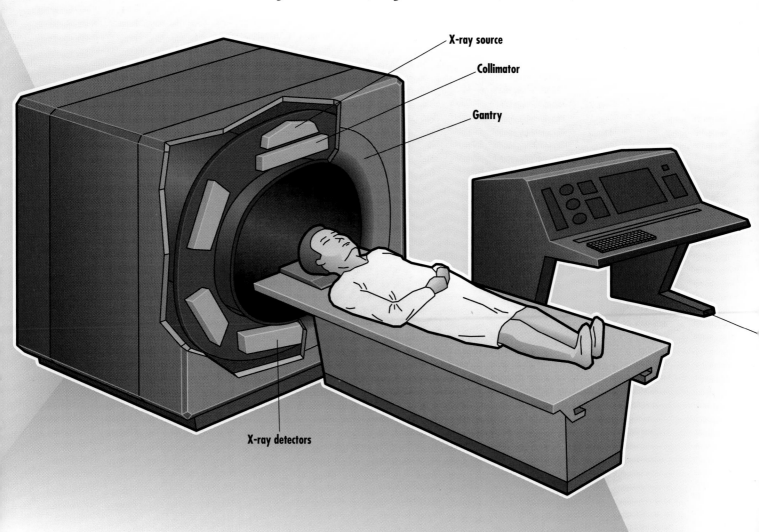

X-ray source

Collimator

Gantry

X-ray detectors

2 The X-ray source is turned on, and up to 200 pencil-thin X-rays are beamed through the patient's body. Detectors on the opposite side of the gantry read the X-ray emissions passing through the body and pass the data to a computer.

3 The gantry rotates slightly and beams X-rays through the patient again. This process is repeated many times as the gantry rotates through a 180-degree arc, providing X-ray absorption data from many different angles. At each position, the data gathered by the X-ray detectors is transmitted to the computer.

4 When the scan is complete, the computer analyzes the strength of the X-rays picked up by each detector at each stop in the gantry's travel and turns the information into a picture depicting a cross-sectional slice of the patient's body. The picture is then displayed on the computer screen, giving the attending physician nearly instantaneous feedback.

How Magnetic Resonance Imaging Works

1 The patient is placed in an MRI machine, which consists of a tube containing a long, cylindrical magnet, coils for sending and receiving radio-frequency (RF) signals, a table for the patient to lie on, and a computer.

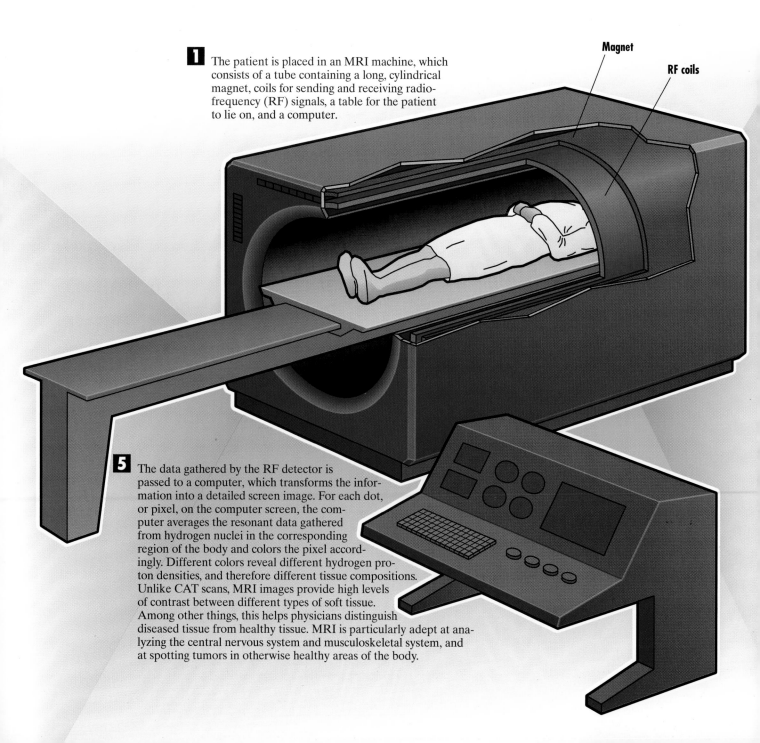

Magnet

RF coils

5 The data gathered by the RF detector is passed to a computer, which transforms the information into a detailed screen image. For each dot, or pixel, on the computer screen, the computer averages the resonant data gathered from hydrogen nuclei in the corresponding region of the body and colors the pixel accordingly. Different colors reveal different hydrogen proton densities, and therefore different tissue compositions. Unlike CAT scans, MRI images provide high levels of contrast between different types of soft tissue. Among other things, this helps physicians distinguish diseased tissue from healthy tissue. MRI is particularly adept at analyzing the central nervous system and musculoskeletal system, and at spotting tumors in otherwise healthy areas of the body.

Magnetic field

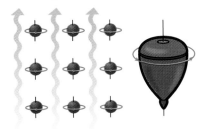

2 The MRI magnet is energized, producing a strong, uniform magnetic field throughout the patient's body. The magnetic field lines up the spinning nuclei of hydrogen atoms in the body so that their spin axes all point in the same direction. (Protons and electrons spin, and it is imbalances in the spin of these charged particles—particularly electrons—that give some elements, such as iron, magnetic properties.) The spin axes line up in the same manner that iron filings do when placed near a magnet. Each nucleus is like a toy top spinning in place about a vertical axis.

Magnetic field

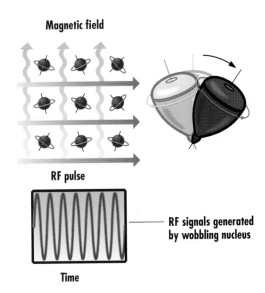

RF pulse

RF signals generated by wobbling nucleus

Time

3 An RF pulse is passed through the MRI chamber to upset the spin axes of the nuclei. In this state, a spinning nucleus wobbles like a top that has been nudged off center, and emits weak RF signals that can be measured by sensitive RF detectors. The nucleus is said to be *resonating*.

Magnetic field

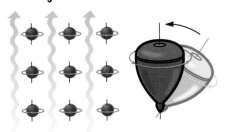

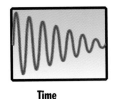

RF signals generated by the nucleus as it realigns itself

Time

4 The RF pulse is turned off and the spinning particles return to their previously aligned states. RF coils inside the MRI machine read RF emissions produced as the spin axes return to normal. The rate of signal decay—the speed at which the nuclei realign themselves in the magnetic field—reflects the varying degrees to which they were deflected by the RF pulse. The measurement of signal decay and other data provide information about tissue composition. Typically, radio signals are applied and removed several times over a period of 10 to 20 seconds, during which the patient must lie as still as possible. Recent advances in MRI technology have improved upon this, reducing scan times to just a few seconds, and, in some cases, even fractions of seconds.

Video Games

The subject of video games hardly demands an introduction. Nearly everyone has played a video game at one time or another, either on a personal computer, a home entertainment system, or a stand-alone game machine such as those found in arcades. Nolan Bushnell of Atari is generally credited with inventing the first video game; he developed Pong, an electronic ping-pong game, in 1973. Since then, video games have grown both in number and sophistication. Popular video games such as Pac-Man and Space Invaders brought video games to the forefront of the computer scene in the late 1970s and early 1980s. Today's video games combine fast, interactive graphics with large-capacity storage devices such as hard disks and CD-ROM drives, which are capable of storing thousands of detailed graphics scenes, to thoroughly stretch the border separating imagination and reality.

The premise behind video games is simple. The player controls the action on the computer screen using an input device such as a joystick, trackball, keyboard, or mouse. The computer program that drives the game translates input into events in the game's simulated environment. For example, pushing a joystick to the left might tell the computer to move an object on the screen to the left. In response, the computer redraws the screen with the object positioned slightly to the left of where it was before. By redrawing the computer screen several times per second and moving the object one increment to the left each time, the computer creates the illusion that the object is moving across the screen. The effect is similar to that of cartoon animation, in which frames, or *cels*, are displayed rapidly in succession to fool the eye into thinking that the image on the screen is moving.

The game software controls everything that happens on the screen. On personal computers, game software is typically stored in *RAM*, or *random-access memory*. Arcade game machines usually store their software in permanently programmed *ROM*, or *read-only memory*. The software used in home entertainment systems is stored in ROM housed in plug-in game cartridges.

In order to understand how video games work, let's examine a fictitious game called Passageways. The object of the game is to guide a player through a maze. Enemies, whose movements are controlled by the computer, rove the maze in an effort to prevent you from reaching the exit. Contact with an enemy "kills" your player and ends the game. If you reach the exit untouched, the enemies are vanquished and you win. Every video game works a little differently (the exact details of a video game's operation are left to the discretion of the programmers who write it, and are somewhat dependent upon the type of computer on which the game is run), but Passageways nonetheless demonstrates many of the basic principles used in modern-day video games.

How Video Games Work

1 The Passageways playing field is a computer screen composed of thousands of tiny dots called picture elements, or *pixels*, each of which can be set to any one of a number of colors. The screen background is black; the walls of the maze are blue. Your player is represented by a yellow circle, enemies by colored squares. Pixels are arranged in rows and columns. The screen is like a graph with x and y axes, with the origin (0,0) at the lower left corner of the screen. Every pixel on the screen, as well as the position of each player, can be identified with an x–y coordinate pair.

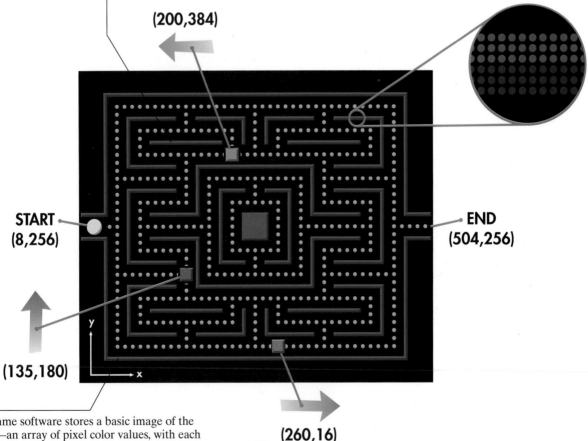

(200,384)

START **(8,256)**

END **(504,256)**

(135,180)

(260,16)

2 The game software stores a basic image of the maze—an array of pixel color values, with each value set to either black or blue—in computer memory (either RAM or ROM). It also stores the x and y coordinates of the endpoints of lines forming an unseen track that runs between the maze walls. By constraining players to travel on the track, the software can force them to move only within the walls, and can detect when the person playing the game has attempted an illegal move by trying to pass through a wall.

3 The x and y coordinates describing each player's position on the screen are stored in RAM. Initially, the yellow player is positioned at the entrance to the maze, and enemies are positioned at strategic locations throughout the maze. The enemies' positions are carefully chosen so that they fall on the path that guides their movements. Each enemy is also assigned a direction vector that specifies whether it is moving up, down, right, or left. The vectors are stored in RAM along with the enemies' positions.

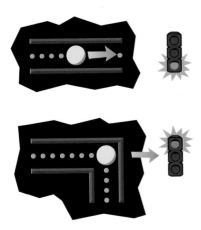

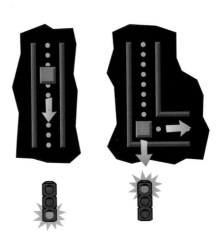

4 Several times each second, the game program reads the input device that guides the yellow player and calculates a new position. If the current position is (98,245) and the input device says move right, the program adds 1 to the player's x coordinate to arrive at a new position of (99,245). This coordinate pair is checked against the endpoint coordinates that define the path between the walls. If the point represented by these coordinates lies on the path, the move is deemed valid and the new coordinates are copied to the RAM location that holds the player's current position. If the point is not on the path, the new coordinates are discarded and the yellow player's position remains the same.

5 The program uses the direction vectors to compute new positions for the enemies. If the red enemy is moving down and its current position is (400,132), the new position is (400,131). As before, the new coordinate pair is checked against the path coordinates and discarded if illegal. Rather than allow the enemy to remain in the same position when a move is ruled invalid, however, the game program examines the path to determine what directions constitute valid moves and picks a new direction vector. (The new vector could be picked at random, or it could be selected pursuant to a set of rules coded into the software. An "intelligent" enemy might pick a vector that takes it toward its prey.) Then the program updates the enemy's position using the new vector information.

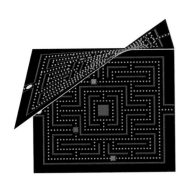

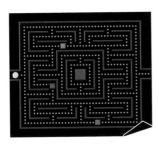

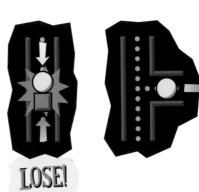

6 The game software redraws the screen using the new player positions stored in RAM. If the video hardware on which the game is running supports an animation technique called double-buffering, the new screen is drawn in the background. When drawing is complete, a hardware toggle displays the new screen by swapping the background screen with the foreground screen (the screen that's visible). The switch occurs almost instantaneously, in the 1/60 of a second or so that it takes for the monitor's sweeping electron beam to complete one full cycle. To the person playing the game, the screen appears unchanged except for the players, which have moved slightly—one pixel, to be exact.

7 The game program compares the yellow player's position to the position of each of the enemies to determine whether a collision has occurred. If the answer is yes, the game ends. If no collision has occurred, the program goes on to see if the yellow player has reached the maze exit. If the player's coordinates are not the same as the exit's coordinates, the program loops back for another iteration; otherwise, it ends the game and either invites you to play again or advances to the next level of the maze. This evaluation process is repeated over and over until a condition is detected that prompts the game's termination.

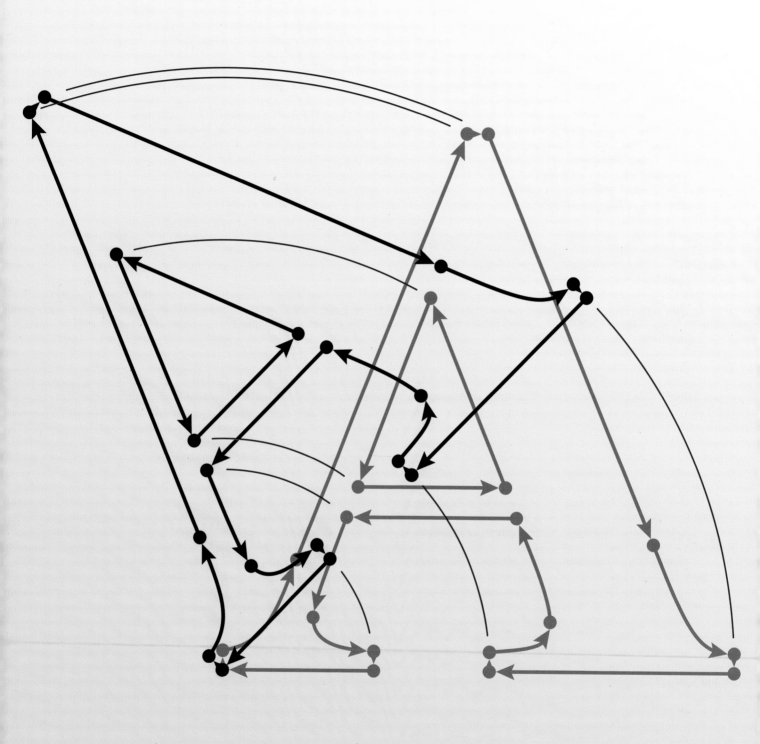

COMPUTER GRAPHICS FUNDAMENTALS

CONTENTS

Chapter 5: Computers, Pixels, and Color
34

Chapter 6: Palettes and Palette Optimization
44

Chapter 7: Drawing, Filling, and Scan Converting
50

Chapter 8: Text and Fonts
60

Chapter 9: Antialiasing
68

IMAGINE HOW DIFFERENT the world would be if computers had no way of drawing pictures on the screen. There would be no flight simulators or CAD systems; no CAT or MRI machines; and no video games. Computers would still be pretty much like they were in the 1940s and 1950s, before there were display screens. It was only in the 1960s that monitors (which at that time were called *video display terminals*, or *VDTs*) started coming around, and it was not until the late 1970s that they saw widespread use. Before the advent of the VDT, computers printed their output on huge, typewriterlike printers called line printers. The computer that historians generally accredit with being the first personal computer—the MITS Altair 8800, introduced in 1975—had neither a monitor nor a printer. It didn't even have a keyboard. You fed instructions into it by flipping switches, and read your output from blinking lights on the front panel.

Today, computers can—and do—draw pictures. It's important to understand how they draw pictures, because it's altogether different from how people do it. First, there's the problem of getting an image onto the screen. A computer screen contains thousands of little dots of light called pixels. To display even the most rudimentary picture, the computer must be able to control the color of each pixel. How does it set one pixel's color to blue while displaying a neighboring pixel in red, white, green, or yellow? Second, there's the matter of organizing pixels into meaningful images. If a computer wants to draw a line or circle on the screen, how does it know which pixels to light up?

The answers to these questions form the foundation for a fundamental understanding of how computer graphics work. In Part 2 of this book, you'll learn how numbers written to a special area of computer memory control the colors of the pixels on the screen. On a simple monochrome system where every pixel is either on or off, writing a 1 to the right place in memory turns a pixel on, and writing a 0 turns it off. On color systems, every color is represented with a number. The number stored in memory for a certain pixel tells the computer's video circuitry what color to display it in. This type of graphics architecture, which is called *memory-mapped video*, is almost universal among computers today. You'll also learn how resolution and colors affect the quality of computer images, and how certain tricks can create the illusion of more colors or enhanced resolution.

Part 2 also discusses how basic shapes such as lines and circles are drawn on the computer screen. A key ingredient in many of these processes is an *algorithm*: a series of instructions that tells a computer how to solve a problem. A line-drawing algorithm tells a computer how to draw a pattern of dots connecting two points to form a straight line; an area-filling algorithm tells it how to fill in an irregularly shaped region with a color. To a large extent, the study of computer graphics is a study of algorithms. Since the 1960s, computer scientists have devised many algorithms to break down complex drawing tasks into simple steps that are repeated over and over. We'll examine some of these algorithms in the chapters that follow.

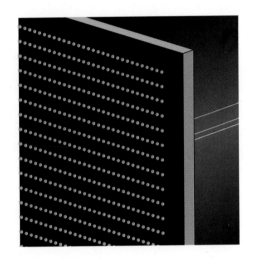

Computers, Pixels, and Color

THE FUNDAMENTAL BUILDING block of all computer images is the picture element, or pixel. A *pixel* is a dot of light on the computer screen that can be set to different colors. Any image, no matter how complex, is really just a collection of pixels. As when applying brush strokes to a fine painting, the trick is to get the right colors in the right places.

Pixels are arranged on the computer screen in rows and columns. The screen's *resolution* is determined by the number of pixels in each row and column. A 640-by-480 screen (a standard resolution on IBM PCs and compatibles equipped with VGA video adapters) displays 640 pixels horizontally and 480 vertically. That may not sound like a lot of pixels, but multiply 640 by 480 and you'll discover that this screen contains more than 300,000 pixels—307,200, to be exact. That's a lot of pixels! Today, 640-by-480 is considered low resolution. Most new PCs are capable of displaying resolutions of 1,024-by-768 or higher, and high-end workstations like those manufactured by Silicon Graphics achieve even higher resolutions.

Each pixel's color can be set independently, but the number of colors that can be displayed on the screen at once may be limited by the graphics hardware that you're using. At one end of the spectrum, you have monochrome systems that display only two colors. At the opposite end, you have *true-color* systems capable of displaying more than 16.7 million colors. Most of the video adapters used in today's personal computers are capable of displaying some number of colors in between. The maximum number of colors that can be displayed simultaneously is determined by the number of data bits set aside for each pixel in a region of memory known as the *video buffer*. On true-color systems, each pixel is represented by 24 bits of color information: eight for the pixel's red component, eight for the green component, and eight for the blue component. Each 8-bit value can hold a number from 0 to 255, with higher numbers corresponding to brighter colors. The fact that a 24-bit value can hold a number as low as 0 and as high as 16,777,215 means that a video adapter that supports 24-bit color can display more than 16.7 million different colors. Various intensities of red, green, and blue can be mixed to produce just about any color under the sun.

The bits representing a pixel in the video buffer don't always specify the pixel's color directly. On a 256-color system, which uses only eight bits per pixel, a value in the video buffer typically identifies one of 256 entries in a table called a *color palette*; the value stored in the palette entry, in turn, determines the color of the pixel. If each palette entry holds 24 bits of color information, the video hardware can still display any color it cares to. The catch is that it can only display 256 different colors at a time. The advantage of a palette-based graphics architecture is that it requires less memory. For a given screen resolution, a true-color video adapter's video buffer must be three times the size of a 256-color video adapter's video buffer.

Regardless of whether a video adapter uses palette-based color or not, the fact remains that a computer graphics program displays colors on the screen by poking values into the video buffer. (For a palette-based device, the program might also poke values into the palette.) If every group of bits were set to the same value, the screen would be all one color. But by varying video buffer values from one pixel to the next, a program can vary the colors of the pixels and form recognizable images on the screen.

As a rule, the more pixels and the more colors a computer can display, the better the quality of the images it can produce. Frequently, however, computer users are faced with a trade-off. The same video adapter than can display 256 colors at a resolution of 1,024-by-768 might display only 16 colors at 1,280-by-1,024. So which is more important: resolution or colors? If the goal is to create photographlike images on the computer screen, the answer is (and this may surprise you) colors. A low-resolution image with 256 colors looks more realistic than a 16-color version of the same image shot at a much higher resolution. This explains why a picture on a television set often looks better than an image on the computer screen. The computer screen might have a higher picture resolution, but a television set is capable of displaying a virtually unlimited number of colors.

One way to make up for a shortage of available colors is to *dither* an image on the computer screen. There are many ways to dither an image, but all of them operate on the same basic principle. The idea is to replace pixels whose colors can't be displayed directly with patterns of pixels whose colors can. Dithering takes advantage of the fact that the human eye will blend adjacent pixels of two different colors and perceive a third color. A dithering algorithm might replace a block of green pixels with a pattern of alternating blue and yellow pixels, a process known as *pattern dithering*. The problem with pattern dithering is that sometimes groups of unrelated pixels combine to form subpatterns called artifacts that distract from the final image. A better way to dither an image is to use a technique called *diffusion dithering*, which does not rely on preset color patterns. Instead, it looks at each pixel in the image, assigns it a new color that matches the original color as closely as possible, performs a simple calculation to quantify the difference between the new color and the old color, and diffuses, or spreads, the difference among the colors of neighboring pixels. For instance, if a pixel's new color contains less red and green than the old color, a diffusion dither would add a little red and green to surrounding pixels. This adaptive approach to dithering eliminates artifacts and generally produces superior results. Dithering can also be used to produce black-and-white renditions of color images for monochrome devices such as printers. A similar process called halftoning is used to create the black-and-white pictures you see in newspapers.

The following illustrations show how images are displayed on the computer screen, how resolution and color affect image quality, how dithering creates the illusion that an image has more colors than it really has, and how a diffusion dither is performed using a simple tool called a Floyd-Steinberg filter.

How Images Are Displayed on the Screen

4 A special device called a digital-to-analog converter (DAC) onboard the video-adapter converts the bits in the video buffer to voltage levels for the monitor's three electron guns. Each electron gun corresponds to one of the three primary colors—red, green, or blue. A separate digital-to-analog conversion is performed for each gun so that the color components of each pixel can be set independently. On palette-based video adapters, the DAC acquires color information from the palette rather than directly from the bits in the video buffer.

3 The inside of the monitor screen is coated with tiny specks of phosphorescent matter called phosphors. Each pixel is composed of three phosphors: one red, one green, and one blue. A phosphor glows when impacted by an electron beam, and stays illuminated for a short period of time (typically a few thousandths of a second) after the electron beam is removed. Various combinations of red, green, and blue phosphor intensities produce various hues and intensities of color.

2 A pixel's color is determined by the bits representing it in the video buffer. By changing the 1s and 0s that represent a pixel in the video buffer, a program running on the computer (such as a word processor or spreadsheet) can change the color of the pixel.

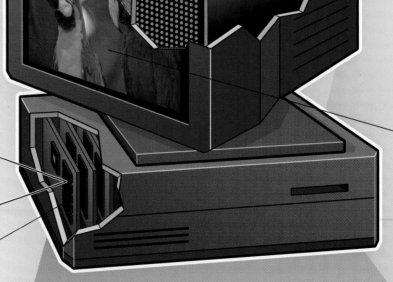

1 The starting point for an image displayed on the computer screen is the video buffer. Most video adapters use a special type of RAM called VRAM (video RAM) for the video buffer. VRAM is similar to common DRAM (dynamic RAM), but it operates slightly faster due to a dual-ported design that permits two devices—the video adapter circuitry that reads video buffer values and converts them to color signals for the monitor, and the computer's CPU, which writes values into the video buffer—to access it simultaneously. A VRAM-based design gives the video hardware a small but perceptible speed boost. It also costs a little more than a video card outfitted with standard DRAM.

5 To illuminate one pixel, the video adapter uses the voltage levels computed by the DAC to drive the output from the monitor's three electron guns. Each gun shoots an electron beam at the screen. The strength of the electron beams, and hence the intensity of the color associated with each gun, is determined by the voltage levels. If a pixel's red component is 255 (the highest value that can be represented with an 8-bit number), the red gun is turned to its highest intensity for that pixel. If the green and blue components are 0, no blue or green colors will be introduced and the pixel will appear on the screen bright red. If, on the other hand, equal amounts of red and blue are introduced and green is again withheld, the pixel will appear magenta.

6 To help target the guns on a particular phosphor, the electron beams pass through holes in a *shadow mask* on their way to the screen. The spacing of the holes determines the spacing of the pixels on the screen, which is commonly referred to as the monitor's dot pitch. A typical monitor has a dot pitch of about .30 millimeters, meaning individual pixels on the screen appear .30 millimeters (slightly more than $\frac{1}{100}$ of an inch) apart.

7 The result of all this is an image on the computer screen. From the standpoint of a graphics program running on the computer, the challenge is to poke the right bit values into the video buffer. The video hardware takes care of the rest. Determining what values to write to the video buffer is what the science of computer graphics is all about: devising methods for translating what we want to see on the screen into discrete sequences of 1s and 0s. For a spreadsheet program drawing blocks of solid colors for a bar graph, the process is relatively straightforward. For a rendering program drawing three-dimensional scenes containing shadows and surface textures, the computations can be quite complex.

8 To paint an entire screen containing hundreds of thousands of pixels, electromagnets inside the monitor deflect the paths of the electron beams so that they sweep across the screen left to right, top to bottom, illuminating every pixel. On non-interlaced systems, the electron beams travel left to right along the first (top) row of pixels to illuminate that row, or *scan line*. Then they jump to the leftmost pixel in the second row and illuminate that row, followed by the third row, the fourth row, and so on. This happens so quickly that the entire screen is painted in about $\frac{1}{60}$ of a second. Because the screen is fully refreshed 60 times per second, we say that it has a *refresh rate* of 60 cycles per second, or 60 Hertz (Hz).

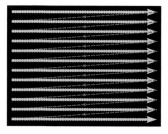

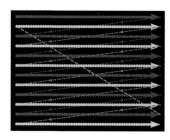

9 On interlaced monitors, odd-numbered scan lines are illuminated in one cycle and even-numbered scan lines in the next. One full screen refresh requires two complete cycles, reducing the monitor's effective refresh rate from 60 screen refreshes per second to 30. Interlaced monitors cost less, but often flicker due to the lower refresh rate.

How Resolution and Color Affect Image Quality

1 It's natural to believe that higher screen resolutions produce better images. And they do—to an extent. For images containing a wide range of colors, however, the number of colors that the video hardware can display at once is more important than the screen resolution. This 450-by-300 screen image was scanned from a photograph. It uses 24-bit color and is hardly, if at all, distinguishable from the original photograph. Now let's see what happens when we reduce the number of colors.

2 When the same image is scanned at the same resolution but with only 256 colors, its quality is degraded slightly but it remains acceptable for most uses. Color shifts are now perceptible. This image exhibits traits of *posterization*, in which pixels of similar but different colors are merged into a single, common color. Posterization is sometimes used for special effects on television and in other visual media, but if it's high image quality you're after, posterization has a debilitating effect.

3 Reducing the number of colors to 16 has a pronounced—and profoundly negative—effect on image quality. Once again, the resolution has not changed. But the 16-color image is a poor stand-in for the original. Subtle differences in color are all but eliminated. Increasing the picture's resolution won't help this situation, because the range of color choices is so limited.

Image courtesy of Eastman Kodak Company

4 Dithering makes the image appear to have more colors than it really has by grouping pixels of different colors close together so that the eye blends them into still more colors. This image contains only 16 colors, and yet its quality is comparable to that of the undithered 256-color image. This is an example of a diffusion dither, which increases the number of perceived colors without the artifacts that are frequently left behind by pattern dithering.

5 When the same image is dithered in 16 colors using a pattern dither instead of a diffusion dither, the results are visibly less attractive. The image is decidedly grainier, and artifacts are clearly visible. Still, pattern dithers are sometimes preferable because they take less time to produce. Some graphics programs use pattern dithers to preview dithered images and diffusion dithers to render the final result.

6 To illustrate the relative importances of resolution and color availability, the original image has been resampled at a resolution of 225 by 150. It now contains exactly one-fourth the pixels of the original, but the overall image quality is only slightly diminished. This is better than any of the versions with fewer colors, despite the decreased resolution. When high image quality is your goal, maximizing the number of available colors is imperative—even if you must sacrifice resolution to achieve it.

How Dithering Works

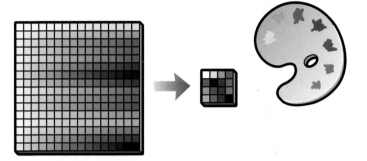

1 A diffusion dither distributes *color error*—the difference between a pixel's actual color and desired color—among all of an image's pixels in such a way that the cumulative color error is zero for the whole picture. Below is a 24-bit image scanned from a photograph. Below that appear 256- and 16-color diffusion-dithered versions of the same image at identical resolutions.

2 The first step in the dithering process is to pick a palette of colors. If the image is being dithered to 16 colors, the dithering software must pick a palette of 16 colors that best represents the range of colors in the image. One way to do this is to count the number of colors actually used in the image and the number of times each color is used, and to pick the 16 most common colors. A better, though more time-consuming, approach involves using a best-fit algorithm to minimize the cumulative difference between the colors in the image and the palette colors. (You'll learn more about this technique in the next chapter.) The palette selection process is critical, because a well-chosen palette produces a correspondingly better dither. Regardless of which method is used, the product of the palette selection process is a set of 16 colors to which every pixel in the final image must conform.

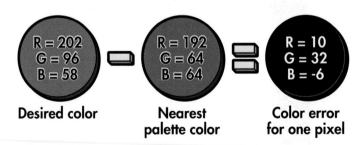

Desired color   Nearest palette color   Color error for one pixel

3 Starting with the first pixel in the image's upper-left corner, the computer picks the palette color that most closely matches the pixel's original color. Suppose that the values of the palette color's red, green, and blue components are 192, 64, and 64, respectively, and that the pixel's original color components are 202, 96, and 58. A color error is computed for each component. In this case, the error in the red component is 202 minus 192, or 10; the error in the green is 32; and the error in the blue is -6. These numbers quantify the difference in what we would like to display for this pixel and what we are able to display.

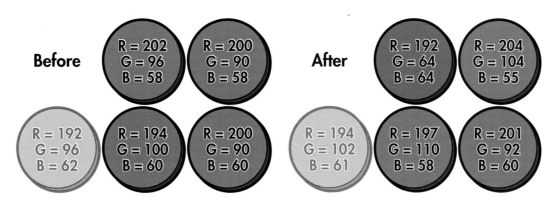

Before
R = 202
G = 96
B = 58

R = 200
G = 90
B = 58

R = 192
G = 96
B = 62

R = 194
G = 100
B = 60

R = 200
G = 90
B = 60

After
R = 192
G = 64
B = 64

R = 204
G = 104
B = 55

R = 194
G = 102
B = 61

R = 197
G = 110
B = 58

R = 201
G = 92
B = 60

4 The error values computed in the previous step are now distributed among neighboring pixels using a *Floyd-Steinberg filter*. The X in the diagram represents the current pixel. The numbers in the surrounding squares represent the fraction of the error that gets added to neighboring pixels. The pixel immediately to the right gets 7/16 of the error; the pixel below and left gets 3/16; the pixel immediately below gets 5/16; and the pixel below and right gets 1/16. The sum of these four fractions is 1, a necessary condition if all the error is to be distributed. These fractions are multiplied by the error values and added to the other pixels. For example, the red component of the pixel to the right is increased by 7/16 of 10, or 5. The green component is increased by 7/16 of 32 (14), and the blue component is decreased by 7/16 of 6 (3). When this step is complete, the pixel in the upper-left corner of the screen has been set to a palette color, and the color values of the three pixels surrounding it (there is no pixel to the left on the row below, so it is ignored) have been modified.

	X	7
3	5	1

Floyd-Steinberg filter

5 The process used to color-map one pixel and apply error values to its neighbors is now repeated in turn for every pixel on the screen. Usually, the software proceeds from left to right, setting each pixel on the row to the nearest palette color and distributing color error among adjacent pixels. When a row is finished, the scan resumes with the leftmost pixel in the next row. Dithering is complete when the pixel in the lower-right corner has been processed.

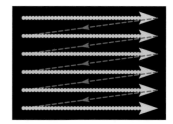

6 An alternative scanning method involves proceeding from left to right for odd-numbered rows and right to left for rows in between, tracing a serpentine path through the image. When the direction is reversed, the template is reversed, too. In the case of the Floyd-Steinberg filter, the 7/16-error term acts on the pixel to the left instead of the pixel to the right when the scan is proceeding from right to left. This winding path through the image yields a slightly different result, but one that might prove superior for some images.

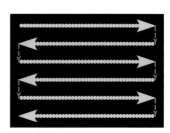

Palettes and Palette Optimization

WHEN PREPARING to paint a picture, an artist assembles a palette of colors to work with. The palette determines the colors that will be applied to the picture. If necessary, additional colors can be created by blending colors from the palette.

Computers also use palettes, but a computer's color palette is more limiting. From the standpoint of a drawing or illustration program laboring to display an image that contains thousands of different colors on graphics hardware that supports at most 256, there's nothing it can do to display more than 256 colors simultaneously. Of course, it can always dither the image. But dithering can only help so much, and even a finely tuned diffusion dither will prove only marginally effective if the palette colors aren't chosen properly. Ultimately, the program must do what it can to ensure that the palette colors match the image colors as closely as possible.

One of the recurring problems in computer graphics is that of selecting a palette of colors with which to display an image whose color count exceeds the palette's color count. What combination of colors will produce the best result? The answer is arrived at through a process called palette optimization. A simple approach to optimizing a palette is to count the number of colors in the image and the number of times that each color is used, and to use the colors that occur the most. If a certain shade of blue occurs 100 times and a particular shade of red occurs only 20, then it obviously makes sense to give the blue priority over the red. But this technique has several drawbacks, one of which is the fact that some colors get eliminated altogether. What happens if the scene is one of a country road that is dominated by blues, yellows, browns, and greens, and a small stop sign appears in one corner? Unless there is enough red elsewhere in the picture to make red one of the chosen colors, the stop sign will be painted some other hue.

It is safer, perhaps, to pick a set of palette colors with evenly distributed red, green, and blue components. This technique ensures a broad spectrum of colors to choose from, but it fails to take into account the fact that most pictures do not contain even color distributions. The stop sign might show up fine, but the subtle variations in the colors of the sky, the trees, and the road could be lost.

An alternative solution is a technique called *median-cut color quantization.* Picture color space as a three-dimensional cube. Each axis of the cube corresponds to one of the three primary colors: red, green, or blue. And each axis is numbered from 0 to 255, with higher numbers representing higher color intensities. You can plot a dot representing a color inside this cube the same way you would plot a point on a three-dimensional graph if you were given the point's x, y, and z coordinates. If the color's red, green, and blue values are 128, 64, and 192, respectively, you could trace outward 128 units on the red axis, 64 units on the green, and 192 units on the blue. Black, whose color components are 0,0, and 0, would fall at one corner of the cube, and white, whose components are 255, 255, and 255, would fall at the corner diagonally opposite. If you plotted a dot for the color of every pixel in a typical true-color image, you'd find that rather than being evenly dispersed throughout the cube, the dots would tend to cluster around certain points.

The median-cut method divides the cube into 256 rectangular volumes containing about the same number of pixels. With color space divvied up this way, the center point of each volume represents an optimal choice for a palette color. Think about it for a moment. In an area of the cube that is dense with dots, there will be more rectangular volumes and a correspondingly larger population of palette colors. Where dots are fewer, palette colors will be fewer also. No color gets ignored completely, but those that occur more frequently get preferential treatment. Using the country road analogy one more time, the median-cut palette colors will be concentrated around blue, yellow, brown, and green, but at least one of them will have enough red in it to approximate the color of the stop sign. Here's how median-cut color quantization works.

How Median-Cut Color Quantization Works

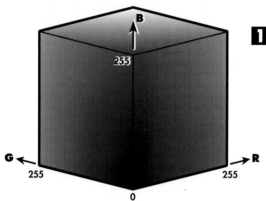

1 A common application for median-cut color quantization is choosing 256 colors to represent a true-color image containing several thousand colors. As an aid in visualizing how the median-cut method works, we'll represent color space with a cube. Each axis corresponds to one of the three primary colors and is numbered from 0 to 255, with higher numbers representing higher color intensities. Colors in the image can be plotted inside the cube like points on a three-dimensional graph.

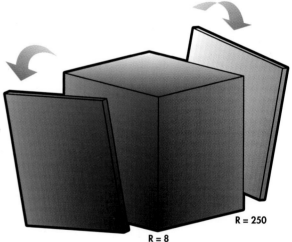

2 The first step is to shave off all ends of the cube that do not contain pixels. If no pixel has a red value less than 8 or greater than 250, for example, then the parts of the cube from R=0 to R=7 and R=251 to R=255 can be discarded.

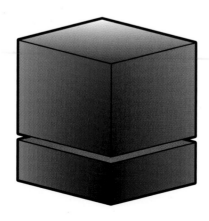

3 The second step is to cut the resulting box in two at the median point of its longest side. If the box's longest side parallels the B axis, the computer picks the median blue value from all the blue values represented in the box (for example, the 50,000th entry in a sorted list of 100,000 blue values) and makes the cut at that point. The box is now divided into two smaller boxes containing equal numbers of pixels.

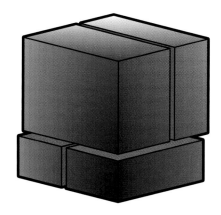

4 This process—trimming the empty ends from the box and performing a median cut along its longest side—is repeated for the two smaller boxes. The original cube is now partitioned into four boxes containing approximately the same number of pixels.

Center point

5 Median cuts are applied repeatedly to divide the cube into 8, 16, 32, 64, 128, and finally 256 boxes. The boxes contain about the same number of pixels, and vary in size in inverse proportion to the pixel density.

6 With color space divided in this manner, picking palette colors is easy. Each of the 256 boxes represents a roughly equal constituency of pixel color values, and the center of each box is an optimal location for a palette color. Given the corner coordinates, simple math yields the coordinates of the center point. (Some graphics programs average all the pixel values in the box rather than compute a center point. This approach takes a little longer but produces an even better palette.) Computing R, G, and B coordinates for all 256 boxes produces 256 representative palette colors.

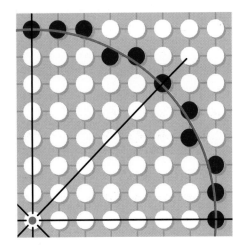

CHAPTER 7

Drawing, Filling, and Scan Converting

LLUMINATING PIXELS ON the computer screen is one thing, but organizing them to present a meaningful picture is quite another. It's rarely enough for a computer just to display pixels. Often those pixels have to be organized to form lines, circles, squares, or other figures. When you did your geometry homework in high school, you drew a line by tracing a pencil along the edge of a ruler. When a computer draws a line, it must cobble together a stair-stepped pattern of pixels that approximates a straight line.

The process by which an idealized form such as a line or circle is transformed into pixels on the computer screen is called *scan conversion*. Over the years, various algorithms have been devised to make the process of scan converting basic geometric entities such as lines and circles as simple, fast, and efficient as possible. The most popular line-drawing algorithm in use today is the *midpoint line algorithm*, which, given the x and y coordinates of a line's endpoints, allows a computer to calculate the x and y coordinates of all the pixels in between. A related algorithm called the *midpoint circle algorithm* generates x,y coordinate pairs for a circle given the coordinates of the circle's center point and a radius. The beauty of these algorithms is that they do not require any fancy computations involving decimals and fractions; they use only whole numbers, and for the most part they rely on simple addition and subtraction. This speeds up the scan conversion process because computers perform integer addition and subtraction very quickly.

Unless you feel like digging into the math behind them (something we definitely won't get into!), the midpoint line and circle algorithms are going to seem a little like black magic. The line algorithm begins by calculating a "magic" number from the coordinates of the line's endpoints. Then it starts at one of the endpoints and travels toward the other, illuminating pixels as it goes. At each stop along the way, another "magic" number is added or subtracted. The sign of the result—whether it is positive or negative—tells the computer which pixel to illuminate next. It's hard to attach any physical significance to the numbers, because they are meaningful only within the context of the algorithm and only in relation to each other. But if you can trust that the underlying theory is sound, you'll have no trouble comprehending how the algorithm itself works.

Another task that computer graphics programs are frequently called upon to perform is a *boundary fill*. Given an arbitrarily shaped region that is bordered by pixels of a certain color, the challenge is to fill it with pixels of another color. The classic way to attack this problem is to set a randomly selected pixel inside the region to the fill color, and then to do the same for the pixel's four neighbors (up, down, right, and left), for the neighbors' neighbors, and so on. Neighboring pixels whose color matches the border color are skipped, so the fill does not spill over the borders. Unfortunately, this approach tends to require lots of memory, and a region containing a few thousand pixels can easily overflow a computer's memory capacity. A better approach—the one used by BASIC's PAINT command, and by many drawing packages that support painting and filling operations—is the *line-adjacency boundary fill algorithm*, which operates on the same principle as the pixel-at-a-time algorithm but uses memory much more judiciously.

The secret to the line-adjacency method is that it deals with rows of pixels rather than individual pixels. Rather than start with one pixel and its neighbors, the line-adjacency algorithm fills an entire row of pixels. Then it fills the rows immediately above and below, and then the rows above and below those, and so on, until the entire bounded region is filled. By biting off bigger chunks of the area that it is asked to fill, the algorithm reduces the number of steps required and shrinks its memory requirements proportionately.

All this talk about algorithms may seem terribly esoteric. After all, how hard can it be to draw a line? A lot of effort has been expended over the years to create the fastest possible scan-conversion and boundary-fill routines. In the world of computers, speed is everything, and a graphics program that is slightly slower than a competitor's might translate into millions of dollars in lost sales. The good news is that if you can add 2 and 2, you can understand how the midpoint line, midpoint circle, and line-adjacency boundary fill algorithms work. Here's a step-by-step description of all three.

How Lines Are Scan Converted into Pixels

1 The starting point for a scan-converted line is a pair of pixels to serve as its endpoints. An ideal line connecting the endpoints is shown in red. The computer's job is to determine which pixels best approximate the ideal line.

(16,10)

3 To begin the scan conversion process, the computer illuminates the pixel that forms the line's left endpoint.

4 After the first pixel is illuminated, the computer moves to the right one unit. Now it must make a decision: Should it illuminate the pixel on the same row as the previous pixel, or the one on the row above? The midpoint line algorithm provides a means for making this decision without resorting to complicated math. The computer simply examines the value of C. If C is less than 0, the pixel on the same row is selected and C is adjusted by adding the length of ruler A; if C is greater than or equal to 0, the pixel on the next higher row is selected and C is adjusted by subtracting the length of ruler B. In effect, the value of C tells the computer which pixel lies closer to the ideal line. In this case, C is less than 0, so the lower of the two pixels is illuminated and A is added to C, yielding 5.

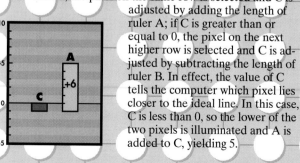

5 The computer steps another pixel position to the right and is once again faced with a decision between two pixels. Since C is now greater than 0, the pixel on the next higher row is illuminated and B is subtracted from C, yielding −3.

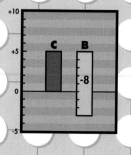

2 As a prelude to the scan conversion process, the computer calculates three values from the endpoints' coordinates. Two of the values will remain the same throughout the scan conversion process. We'll represent them with rulers, which we'll call ruler A and ruler B. The length of ruler A is two times the difference in the endpoints' y coordinates, which in this example equals 6. The length of ruler B is two times the number you get when you subtract the difference in the endpoints' y coordinates from the difference in the end-points' x coordinates, or 8. The third value, which we'll call C, is computed by multiplying the difference in the y coordinates by two and subtracting the difference in the x coordinates. The value of C will change as the algorithm progresses, so we'll represent it with a bar on a bar graph. Initially, C is equal to –1.

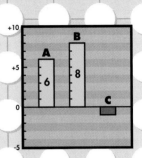

6 This procedure—move one place to the right, choose a pixel based on the value of C, and adjust C accordingly—is repeated until the right endpoint is reached. The line has now been scan converted into pixels. The scan conversion process is laborious if done by hand, but for computers, which excel at simple, repetitive operations, it's a snap. And because the repetitive part of the process requires nothing more than simple addition and subtraction (something else computers excel at), lines can be drawn exceedingly fast.

(23,13)

7 Geometric figures such as triangles and squares can be scan converted from individual line segments. To draw a triangle, the computer performs three separate scan conversions: one for each leg of the triangle. Polygons with any number of sides can be drawn this way. The mechanics of the midpoint line algorithm change slightly if the line doesn't lie between –45 and 45 degrees, but the principle is the same in all cases.

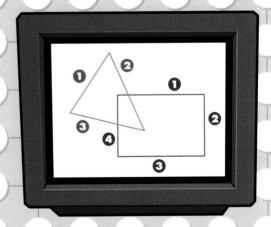

How Circles Are Scan Converted into Pixels

1 The starting point for a circle is a center point and a radius. A perfect circle with a radius of seven pixels drawn about the center point (16,10) is shown in red. The computer's job is to determine which pixels best approximate the perfect circle.

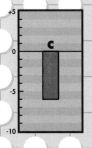

2 Before it begins lighting pixels, the computer performs a simple calculation. It computes a number that we'll call C by subtracting the circle's radius from the number 1. Since the radius is 7, C is equal to –6. As in the previous example, C, whose value will change as the scan conversion progresses, will be represented by a vertical bar.

3 To begin scan converting the circle into pixels, the computer illuminates the pixel at the topmost point on the circle. Since the center point is (16,10) and the circle's radius is 7, the topmost pixel lies at (16,17).

4 Now the computer moves right one pixel position and faces a choice between two pixels: the pixel on the same row as the previous pixel, or the one on the row below. The value of C tells it which one to pick. If C is less than 0, the pixel on the same row is selected and C is modified by adding 3 plus two times the difference between the previous pixel's x coordinate and the center point's x coordinate. If C is greater than or equal to 0, the pixel on the next lower row is chosen and C is modified by subtracting the difference between the previous pixel's x coordinate and the center point's x coordinate from the difference between the previous pixel's y coordinate and the center point's y coordinate, multiplying by 2, subtracting 5, and subtracting the result from C. (The values used to modify C aren't calculated ahead of time as they are when scan converting a line, because they, like C, change as the algorithm progresses.) In this example, C is less than 0, so it is modified by adding 3+(2×0), or 3. The upper pixel is illuminated and C's value is now –3.

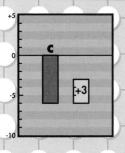

5 The computer moves right another unit and repeats the previous step. C is still less than 0, so again the pixel on the same row is illuminated and C is modified by adding 3+(2×1). C's new value is 2.

6 When this procedure is repeated for the next position, C is greater than 0 and the pixel on the lower row is illuminated. The circle has now started its downward turn toward the x axis. C is modified this time by subtracting (2×(7–2))-5. C's new value is –3, so the next pixel will have the same y value as this one.

7 The procedure is re-peated until one-eighth of the circle is completed. To quickly fill in the remaining seven-eighths of the circle, the computer mirrors the completed pixels about the x and y axes, and about a pair of imaginary axes that run through the origin at 45-degree angles. To fill in the remainder of the circle's upper-right quadrant, for example, the computer mirrors the existing pixels about the 45-degree line passing through the center of the quadrant. The result is a complete image of a circle that is perfectly symmetric.

How Bordered Regions Are Filled

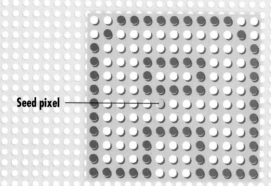

Seed pixel

1 Suppose a computer is asked to fill an arbitrary region bordered by blue pixels with red pixels. At the outset, it has just one piece of information to work with: the coordinates of a *seed pixel*, which lies somewhere (anywhere) inside the region. This is a perfect job for a line-adjacency boundary fill algorithm.

2 To begin the filling process, the computer scans left and right on the row that contains the seed pixel, filling in red pixels as it goes until a blue border pixel is encountered. When this step is completed, the row containing the seed pixel has been filled with red.

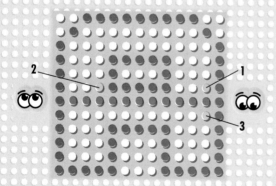

3 The computer examines the row above the current row and the row below. Each is scanned from right to left and the coordinates of any pixel that lies just left of a blue border pixel and hasn't already been turned red is saved in memory. We'll call these *edge pixels* in order to distinguish them from border pixels. In this example, two edge pixels are identified on the upper row (pixels 1 and 2) and one is identified on the bottom row (pixel 3). The numbers reflect the order in which the edge pixels were identified. Pixel 1 was identified first, pixel 2 second, and pixel 3 third.

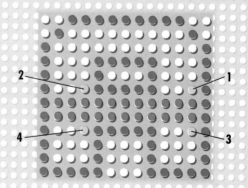

4 Now the computer repeats the two previous steps for the highest-numbered edge pixel, which at the moment is pixel 3. In effect, the algorithm is repeated with pixel number 3 serving as the seed pixel. Upon completion, the row below the one we started with is completely filled in and two new edge pixels have been identified on the next row down. The former pixel number 3 has already been processed, leaving only the coordinates of pixels 1 and 2 saved in memory, so the new edge pixels are assigned the numbers 3 and 4.

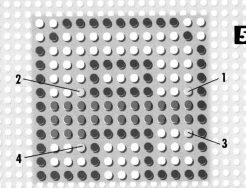

5 The fill algorithm is repeated yet again with pixel 4 as the seed pixel. This fills in the top row of the left leg of the figure, and identifies a new pixel 4 on the next lower row.

6 This process is repeated over and over until there are no more edge pixels remaining to be processed. This sequence of illustrations documents the algorithm's progression through the region, row by row. Notice what happens between *b* and *c*, when the left leg has been filled in and a scan of the adjacent rows turns up no more edge pixels. At this moment, the only pixel addresses remaining in storage are those of the pixels labeled 1, 2, and 3 in the previous illustration. Since pixel 3 is now the highest-numbered edge pixel, the computer jumps to the row containing pixel 3.

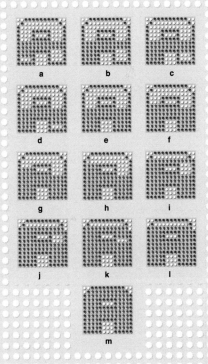

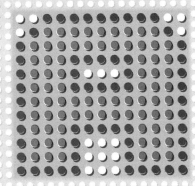

7 When there are no more edge pixels remaining to be processed, the algorithm ends, and the region has been filled completely with red pixels. The line-adjacency algorithm is suitable for filling any enclosed region, including regions with holes (also called *islands*) and legs like the one shown here. And because it processes an entire row in each phase of operation, the line-adjacency fill is faster and less memory-intensive than is a classic boundary fill algorithm that processes just one pixel at a time.

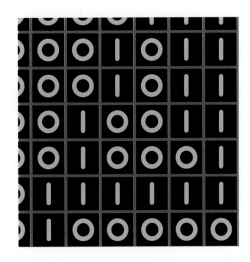

Text and Fonts

F LINES AND CIRCLES were all a computer was ever called upon to draw, life as a computer would be boring indeed. But because humans communicate with the printed word, computers are required to draw letters, numbers, and other textual symbols as well. Text presents something of a challenge, because a single character might contain dozens of tiny lines and curves carefully chosen to achieve a certain stylistic look. Look closely at the text on this page. A lowercase *s* has tiny tails (called *serifs*) at both ends, and its thickness, or *stroke width*, varies from thin at the top and bottom to relatively thick in the middle. Somehow these details must be represented in a form that a computer can both understand and reproduce.

A set of characters that share similar visual characteristics is called a *font*. Characters of a particular font are all in the same typeface family, at the same size, and with the same attributes (such as bold or italic). For example, the characters in the chapter title on this page and the running head on the previous page are both members of the Futura Condensed typeface family, but they do not belong to the same font because the chapter title is in a larger point size and is in boldface.

One way to represent the characters in a font is to store images of them as bitmaps in which the dots that make up the letter *A*, for example, are represented by bits of data whose value is 1, and the empty space in and around the letter by bits whose value is 0. Fonts stored in this manner are called *bitmapped fonts*. Bitmapped fonts are quick to draw, but they tend to require lots of storage space. A bitmapped font containing 256 characters, each drawn in a 24-by-16 grid of pixels, requires about 12 kilobytes to store on a disk. If you need ten different point sizes (font heights are measured in *points*, where 1 point equals ½ of an inch), you need ten bitmapped fonts. And if you want bold, italic, and bold-italic versions of all ten point sizes, you need a total of 40 different fonts.

Outline fonts store mathematical descriptions of the characters rather than dot-by-dot replicas. Outline fonts require more time to display and print than do bitmapped fonts because the dot patterns must be calculated from the outline formulas, but they are vastly more flexible. A character in an outline font can be scaled to any size. Because the computer is scaling outlines and not dots, there is no loss of definition in going from one point size to another—a 72-point character looks as good as a 10-point character. (A 10-point bitmapped character scaled to 72 points would be severely stair-stepped, the result of magnifying the image with no accompanying increase in resolution.) Furthermore, outline fonts can be rotated for special effects such as text printed at an angle or along a curve. One outline font can take the place of dozens of bitmapped fonts, and can do things a bitmapped font never dreamed of. PostScript fonts are outline fonts; so are TrueType fonts. These fonts are the wave of the future, and are already used on everything from the fastest computer graphics workstations to inexpensive personal computers.

The following pages illustrate how computers draw fonts of both varieties.

How Bitmapped Fonts Work

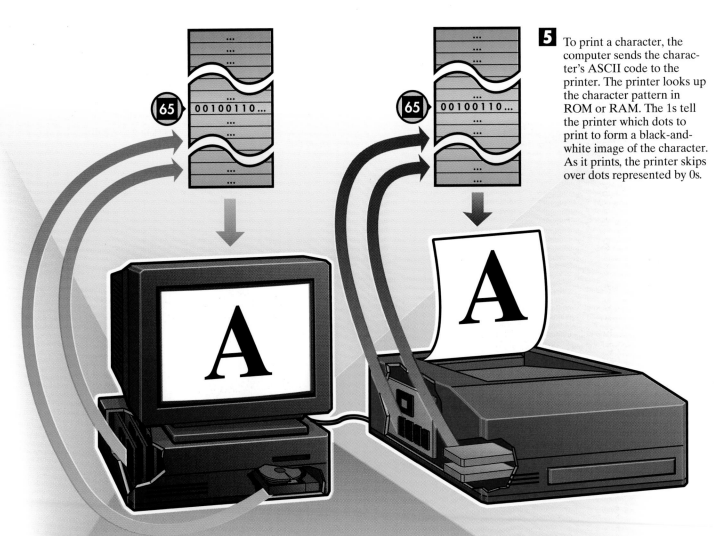

5 To print a character, the computer sends the character's ASCII code to the printer. The printer looks up the character pattern in ROM or RAM. The 1s tell the printer which dots to print to form a black-and-white image of the character. As it prints, the printer skips over dots represented by 0s.

3 Bitmapped screen fonts are usually copied to the computer's RAM from the hard disk, or stored in ROM on the video adapter. To display a character on the screen, the computer uses the character's ASCII code to find the corresponding pattern of 1s and 0s in the table. Then it uses that pattern to draw the character, one pixel at a time, on the screen. A 1 tells the computer to illuminate the corresponding pixel; a 0 tells it to leave the pixel as is, or to set it to the color of the screen's background.

4 Bitmapped printer fonts are frequently stored in ROM inside the printer or in font cartridges plugged into the printer. They can also be downloaded to some printers via the same serial or parallel port connection used to transmit character codes and printer commands. These fonts are often called *downloadable fonts* or *soft fonts*, and are stored in font files on a computer's hard disk. Once downloaded, they reside in RAM inside the printer. Unless the printer's RAM happens to be nonvolatile (meaning it doesn't lose its information when power is turned off), soft fonts must be downloaded anew each time the printer is started.

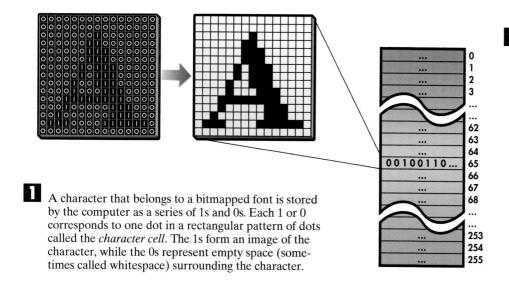

1 A character that belongs to a bitmapped font is stored by the computer as a series of 1s and 0s. Each 1 or 0 corresponds to one dot in a rectangular pattern of dots called the *character cell*. The 1s form an image of the character, while the 0s represent empty space (sometimes called whitespace) surrounding the character.

2 The groups of 1s and 0s making up the characters that constitute a font are arranged in tabular form. For a font containing 256 different characters, the table contains 256 entries. A character is identified with a number from 0 to 255 that indexes an entry in the table. Most fonts use the ASCII (American Standard Code for Information Interchange) numbering system for the letters of the alphabet, the numerals 0 through 9, and punctuation symbols. The ASCII code 65, for example, corresponds to a capital *A*.

6 The preferred way to display a bold or italicized version of a bitmapped character is to use separate fonts containing bitmaps of bold and italic characters. When bold and italic fonts are not available, a computer might form a rough approximation of them by applying a few simple tricks to the base character patterns. The example at right shows how an italicized *A* can be created from a normal *A* by shifting rows of pixels and increasing the magnitude of the shift as the distance from the character's baseline increases. Rows 4 through 6 are shifted to the right one pixel, rows 7 through 9 two pixels, and rows 10 through 12 three pixels. Note the resulting discontinuity in the letter's left stem and the jagged right edge of the right stem.

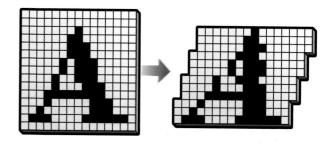

7 Bitmapped fonts can be scaled to larger sizes by replicating pixels both horizontally and vertically, but the results are rarely pleasing. Characters enlarged from bitmaps have a crude, stair-stepped look. The better solution is to have a separate font for each point size so characters will be properly formed regardless of height and width.

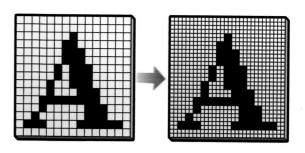

How Outline Fonts Work

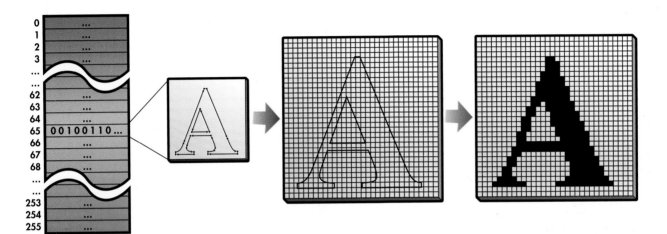

1 Characters that belong to an outline font are arranged in tables like bitmapped fonts, but the table entries do not contain bitmapped images of the characters. Instead, they contain mathematical descriptions of the character outlines that permit characters to be scaled to any size. A character description is essentially a set of statements that tells the computer how to draw a series of connecting lines and curves that form the character outline.

2 To draw a character, a piece of software called an *interpreter* reads and executes the statements. The result is a character outline scaled to the desired size. On systems that run Windows and use TrueType fonts, the interpreter is built into the operating system. On computers that utilize third-party font managers such as Adobe Type Manager, the interpreter is part of the font manager.

3 After scaling is complete, a component of the interpreter called the *rasterizer* or *scan converter* decides which pixels to illuminate based on the shape described by the font outline. The scan conversion process can be as simple as illuminating all the pixels whose centers fall on or inside the character outline. Sometimes special considerations must be made, such as ensuring that all three legs of a lowercase *m* are the same width even if the character outline falls in such a way that one leg covers more pixel centers than the others. Font instructions to eliminate these irregularities, which are more pronounced at smaller scales, are called *hints*.

4 Simple geometric transforms allow outline fonts to be rotated to any angle. To rotate an *A* counterclockwise 45 degrees, the interpreter recomputes the positions and orientations of the lines and curves before drawing the outline. Then it performs a routine scan conversion to fill in the dots.

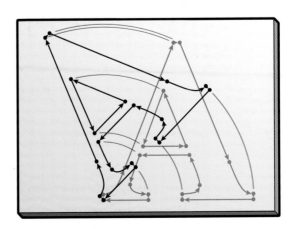

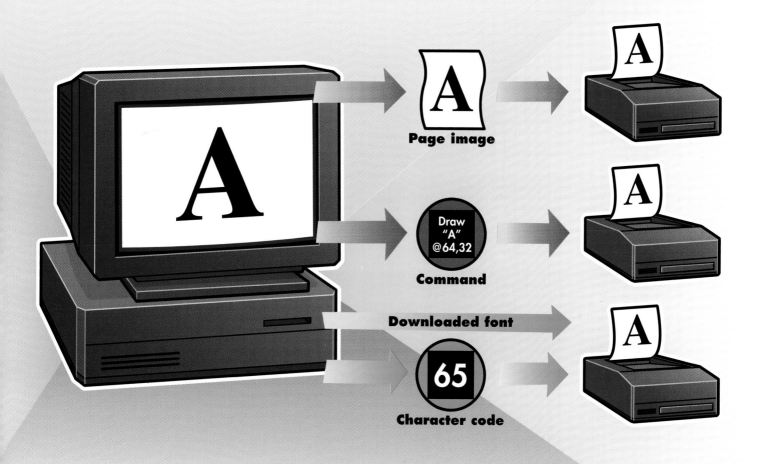

Page image

Command

Downloaded font

Character code

5 If output is going to the printed page rather than to the screen, the scan converter may assemble a complete image of the page from the scan-converted font outlines and send it to the printer all at once. Some printers have outline fonts and font interpreters built in, in which case the computer can send simple commands to the printer and let the printer do the work of transforming the commands into printable characters. On printers that support soft fonts but lack font interpreters, another option is to let the computer's scan converter generate bitmaps for all the characters and download the resulting bitmapped font to the printer prior to printing anything. This speeds up the printing process by performing all the scan conversions ahead of time and allowing the computer to transmit simple character codes.

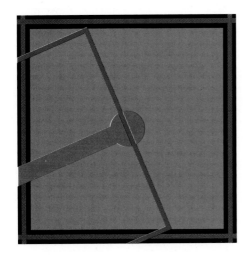

CHAPTER 9

Antialiasing

ONE PROBLEM THAT'S just about certain to come up when scan converting lines, circles, and text on the computer screen is jagged, stair-stepped edges. This effect, which is known as *aliasing*, is a natural—and unfortunate—consequence of our all-or-nothing approach to illuminating pixels. A conventional line-drawing algorithm either turns pixels on or leaves them turned off. At higher resolutions, when pixels on the computer screen are so close together that it's difficult to distinguish between them, aliasing effects are barely noticeable. But at lower resolutions, aliasing gives an image a harsh, computerized look. The coarser the resolution, the more pronounced the stair-stepping becomes and the less realistic a scan-converted image looks.

A solution to this problem comes in the form of a technique called antialiasing. *Antialiasing* takes advantage of the fact that pixels can be set to various intensities, and that if the intensities of adjoining pixels are properly manipulated, they will blend to form a smooth image. A computer can't turn on part of a pixel, but it can display it at less than maximum intensity. Unlike the midpoint line algorithm, which examines pairs of pixels that the ideal line passes between and illuminates one in each pair, an antialiasing scan conversion algorithm illuminates both. Neither pixel, however, is set to its highest intensity. If the ideal line passes midway between two pixels, each pixel is shown at half its normal intensity. If the line passes closer to one pixel than the other, the nearer of the pixels is displayed proportionally brighter than the more distant one. The only time that a pixel is displayed at maximum intensity is when the ideal line passes exactly through its center.

That's one approach to calculating the intensity values of individual pixels forming a straight line. A slightly different one that is widely used in commercial graphics programs assumes that a line has a thickness that is equal to the width of one pixel; the program then determines each pixel's intensity based on how much of the pixel is covered by the line.

Antialiased lines tend to look a little blurry, but that's what antialiasing does: It selectively blurs an image to hide discontinuities. You sacrifice clarity, but you get back quality. Moreover, entire images can be antialiased, and at least one popular video adapter displays antialiased fonts in Microsoft Windows. Antialiasing can be accomplished in a variety of ways, but the results are all very much the same: higher-quality images that minimize the negative impact of translating lines, circles, and other continuous forms into dot patterns on the computer screen. Here's how antialiasing works.

How Antialiasing Works

1 A conventional line-drawing algorithm scan converts a straight line by turning on pixels along an ideal line connecting the endpoints. Here, the ideal line appears in red, and each square in the grid represents one pixel. At each unit increment along the horizontal, the pixel whose center lies closest to the red line is turned to fullest intensity. Other pixels remain turned off.

2 An antialiasing scan converter sets pixels along the line to various intensities so that the eye will see a more or less continuous image. The ideal line appears in red and a rectangle representing a 1-pixel-wide version of the line appears in blue. Each pixel is illuminated according to the percentage of its square that is covered by the blue box. Pixels that are covered more fully get turned on the brightest, while those that are covered the least get illuminated proportionally less. One small deficiency of this technique is that it doesn't take into account where the area formed by the intersection of the rectangle and the square lies in relation to the pixel's center point; a small area at the fringe of a square contributes as much to the pixel's brightness as an equally sized area near the center. Some antialiasing routines compensate for this by allowing areas nearer the center to contribute more heavily to the pixel's brightness, producing even better looking lines.

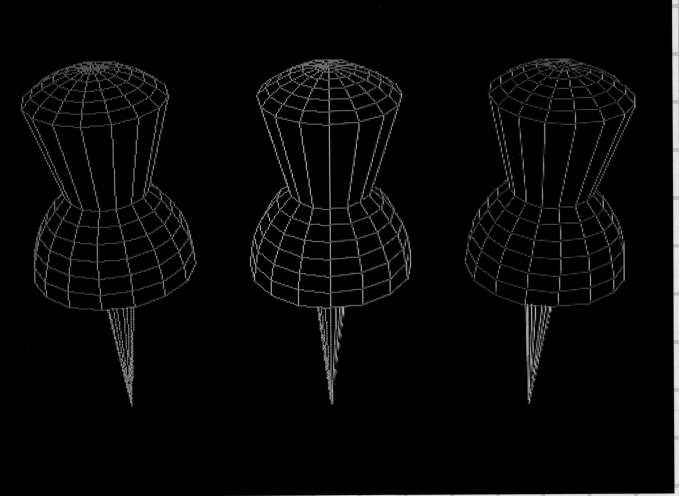

3 The lines in the left half of this image are aliased, and those in the right half are antialiased. Antialiased lines generally take longer to draw than aliased lines because the computer has to perform more computations. As this illustration shows, however, the resulting image quality often justifies the extra time.

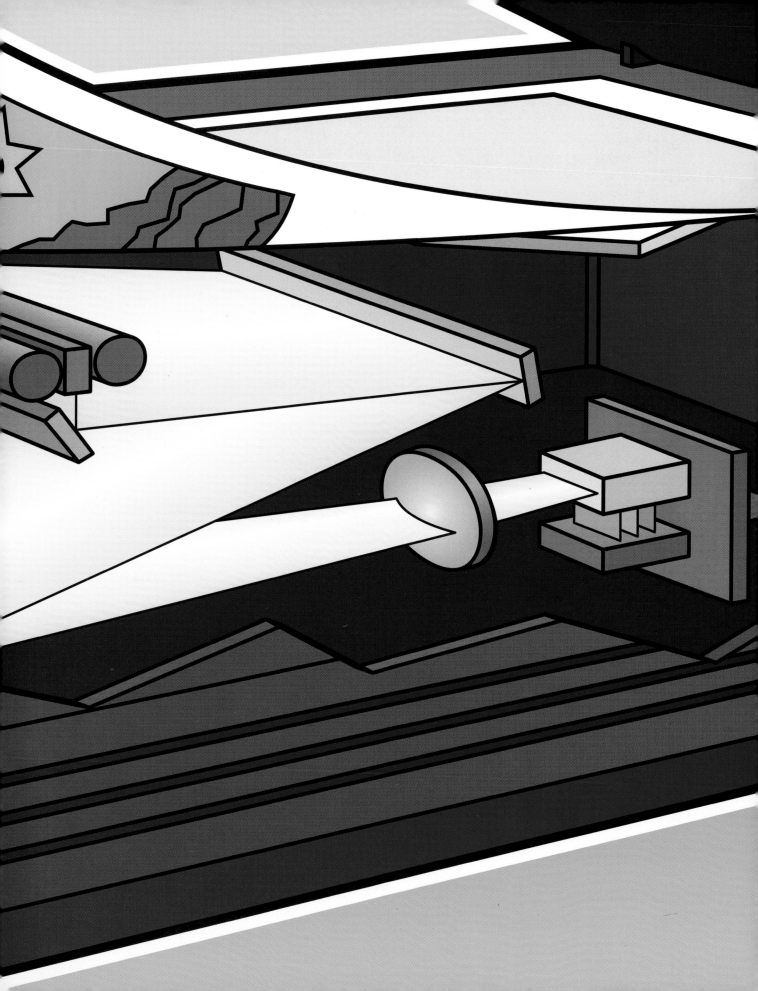

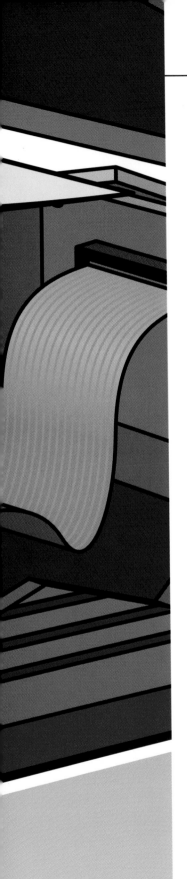

IMAGES AND IMAGE PROCESSING

C O N T E N T S

Chapter 10: Getting Images into the Computer
76

Chapter 11: Bitmapped File Storage
84

Chapter 12: Image Compression
90

Chapter 13: Image Enhancement and Special Effects
98

OVERVIEW

ONE OF THE hottest areas of computer graphics these days is digital image processing. Image processing software lets you electronically manipulate pictures captured by scanners, digital cameras, and other input devices. Once an image is transformed into so many pixels on the screen, the computer can do things with it that are difficult or impossible to do on film: change colors, blur and sharpen edges, combine images to form composite photographs, and a whole lot more. It can even add special effects. One of the most dazzling image processing effects is embossing, which makes an ordinary image look as if it had been molded in metal. Another converts a still photograph into a watercolor look-alike. Perhaps surprisingly, such effects are not difficult to achieve. A handful of easy-to-understand algorithms lies at the core of many of the marvelous tricks that you see on the computer screen.

Image processing isn't all fun and games; it has serious applications, too. Long before it became a pursuit for the masses, image processing was used to sharpen photographs transmitted from defense satellites. Today, popular software packages such as Adobe Photoshop and Aldus PhotoStyler make it easy for people with personal computers to try their hand at electronic photo wizardry. Combine one of these packages with an inexpensive color scanner, a digital camera, or a Kodak Photo CD-compatible CD-ROM drive, and you have everything you need to set up shop. Image processing software works best on computers with 24-bit color. A typical photograph, after all, contains a continuous range of colors with lots of subtle variations. But most image processing programs do an acceptable job on machines with as few as 256 displayable colors by dithering.

In Part 3, we'll take a look at the fast-growing field of computerized image processing, starting with two ways to get images into the computer. From there, we'll see how images are stored on a computer disk and look inside one of the most common bitmapped file formats. Next comes image compression, an amazing technology that whittles large graphics files down to size so more of them can fit on a disk. The best comes last: a behind-the-scenes look at how Photoshop, PhotoStyler, and other image processing programs perform some of their neatest tricks, including blurring, sharpening, and—you guessed it!—embossing.

Getting Images into the Computer

BEFORE YOU CAN use image processing software to manipulate an image, you must get the image into a computer. These days there is no shortage of ways to do that. If you have a camera, you can take a snapshot and send the film off for Kodak Photo CD processing. You'll get back a compact disc containing digital images of your photographs. If the image you want to capture has already been photographed, you can scan it in. Or if you're one of the lucky few who owns a digital camera, you can snap a photograph and transfer it directly to your PC—no fuss, no muss, and no waiting for film to be developed.

A digital camera is a small computer in its own right. A key element in its design is an array of extremely light-sensitive cells on a chip called a *charge-coupled device*, or *CCD*. Light coming into the camera is focused on the CCD, which converts the intensity of the light striking individual cells into analog voltage levels. These voltage levels are converted to digital form and eventually transferred to the computer. Many digital cameras contain DRAM (dynamic random-access memory, the type of RAM used in most computers) or miniature hard disks that retain several images so they can be transferred as a group. Some even use flash memory, which is similar to common DRAM but, like a hard disk, requires no battery power for long-term storage. Images stored in flash memory can be retained for months, even years. Images stored in DRAM, by contrast, are only good as long as there is battery power available. Wait too long to transfer them, and you'll get the pleasure of shooting them again.

Scanners are considered less exotic because they've been around longer, but the technology behind them is no less marvelous. In a flatbed scanner, a scan head travels the length of the page, illuminating it with a bright light. A system of mirrors gathers the light reflected off a narrow strip of the page and directs it through a lens to a row of light-sensitive CCD cells. As in the camera, these cells build up small electrical charges proportional to the intensity of the light striking them. The voltage levels produced by these charges are translated into one row of pixel data. Rows are combined to form a complete image of the page. Hand-held scanners work in much the same way, but of course their mechanics are very different.

Eight-bit gray-scale scanners and cameras translate the intensity of the light striking each cell into a number from 0 to 255. The number 0 corresponds to black, 255 corresponds to white, and numbers in between correspond to shades of gray. Color scanners and cameras separate light into red, green, and blue components before it reaches the CCD. Eight-bit values for red, green, and blue are then combined to form 24-bit color values.

There are many ways to separate the light. A common method on digital cameras involves covering the CCD with a filter containing thousands of tiny colored dots arranged in a precise pattern. Each dot overlays one CCD cell and allows only red, green, or blue light to pass through. Some color scanners make three separate passes over the page, each time illuminating the page with only red, green, or blue light, or using filters to block all but the red, green, or blue components of white light. A few color scanners read the page in one pass by alternating red, green, and blue lights or filters as the scan head travels down the page. The most sophisticated one-pass color scanners use a prism or a prismlike optical device called a *trichroic beam splitter* to separate the colors. The individual beams are then routed to three separate rows of CCD cells, producing a superb color image free of the small irregularities frequently evident in images produced by lesser scanners.

How Digital Cameras Work

1 Light coming into the camera is focused so that it forms an image on the surface of the CCD chip.

← 1 0 0 1 1 1 0 1 0 0 1

7 The image data is transferred from the camera to a computer, usually via a serial port or SCSI (Small Computer System Interface) connection. Once the image resides on the computer, it can be viewed and manipulated with image processing software.

6 The image data is transferred to a local storage medium inside the camera, which typically consists of common DRAM, flash memory, or a miniature hard disk.

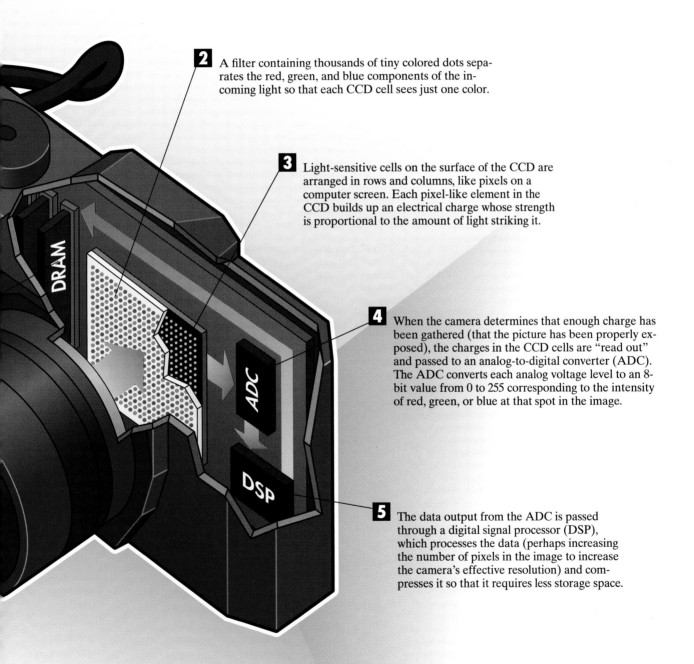

2 A filter containing thousands of tiny colored dots separates the red, green, and blue components of the incoming light so that each CCD cell sees just one color.

3 Light-sensitive cells on the surface of the CCD are arranged in rows and columns, like pixels on a computer screen. Each pixel-like element in the CCD builds up an electrical charge whose strength is proportional to the amount of light striking it.

4 When the camera determines that enough charge has been gathered (that the picture has been properly exposed), the charges in the CCD cells are "read out" and passed to an analog-to-digital converter (ADC). The ADC converts each analog voltage level to an 8-bit value from 0 to 255 corresponding to the intensity of red, green, or blue at that spot in the image.

5 The data output from the ADC is passed through a digital signal processor (DSP), which processes the data (perhaps increasing the number of pixels in the image to increase the camera's effective resolution) and compresses it so that it requires less storage space.

How Scanners Work

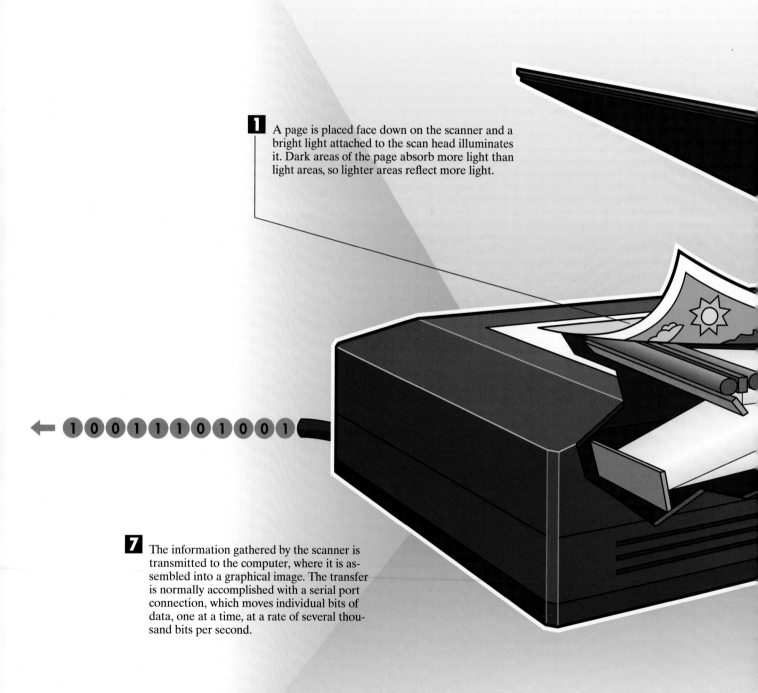

1 A page is placed face down on the scanner and a bright light attached to the scan head illuminates it. Dark areas of the page absorb more light than light areas, so lighter areas reflect more light.

1 0 0 1 1 1 0 1 0 0 1

7 The information gathered by the scanner is transmitted to the computer, where it is assembled into a graphical image. The transfer is normally accomplished with a serial port connection, which moves individual bits of data, one at a time, at a rate of several thousand bits per second.

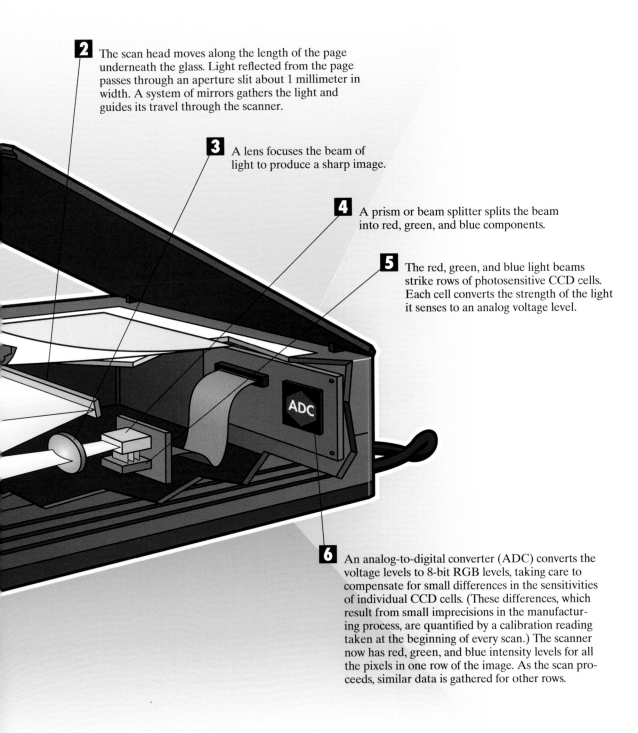

2 The scan head moves along the length of the page underneath the glass. Light reflected from the page passes through an aperture slit about 1 millimeter in width. A system of mirrors gathers the light and guides its travel through the scanner.

3 A lens focuses the beam of light to produce a sharp image.

4 A prism or beam splitter splits the beam into red, green, and blue components.

5 The red, green, and blue light beams strike rows of photosensitive CCD cells. Each cell converts the strength of the light it senses to an analog voltage level.

6 An analog-to-digital converter (ADC) converts the voltage levels to 8-bit RGB levels, taking care to compensate for small differences in the sensitivities of individual CCD cells. (These differences, which result from small imprecisions in the manufacturing process, are quantified by a calibration reading taken at the beginning of every scan.) The scanner now has red, green, and blue intensity levels for all the pixels in one row of the image. As the scan proceeds, similar data is gathered for other rows.

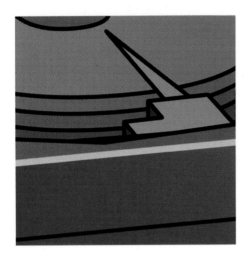

Bitmapped File Storage

I F YOU RUMMAGE through the hard disk of a typical PC, you'll probably find lots of files with extensions like BMP, PCX, GIF, TIF, and JPG. In all likelihood, these files contain bitmapped graphics images. The file name extension reveals the format that the information is stored in. BMP, for example, identifies a BMP file native to Windows and OS/2 (BMP is short for bitmap); TIF is short for TIFF, which stands for Tagged Image File Format. These are but two of the many popular graphics file formats used on personal computers.

Each of these formats has a different way of storing graphical information, and each was designed to suit a particular purpose. The GIF (Graphics Interchange File) format, for example, was contrived to pack as much information into as small a space as possible to reduce download time for CompuServe users. The PCX format was originally put together to store black-and-white graphics files created by an early IBM PC paint program called PC Paintbrush. PCX has been enhanced over the years to handle color and is now a public standard of sorts, widely supported by graphics programs of all types.

What is inside a bitmapped graphics file? Such a file usually contains two types of information: graphical and nongraphical. The graphical data specifies the colors of the pixels; the nongraphical data consists of other information needed to restore the image, such as its height and width. (If an image contained 1 million pixels, how would a graphics program know whether its dimensions were 1,000 by 1,000 or 500 by 2,000?) The nongraphical data may include other information as well, such as a version number or the text of a copyright notice. It all depends on the format, and on who—or what software package—created the file.

Bitmapped files generally use one of two methods to store pixel data. For true-color images, in which any pixel can be set to any one of more than 16 million colors, the color of a pixel is usually stored as a 24-bit value—eight bits each for red, green, and blue. If the image contains 1 million pixels, then the file size will be 3 million bytes plus the length of the nongraphical data. If the image is limited to 256 or fewer colors, however, color information is normally encoded using a palette. Rather than specify a pixel color directly, the value stored for a pixel identifies an entry in a color palette; the palette entry, in turn, identifies the color. This decreases the file size (always a worthy accomplishment, because storage space isn't free) by reducing the number of bits required to represent the color of one pixel.

As an example, suppose a 1-million-pixel image contains 256 different colors. Encoding each pixel color as a 24-bit color value results in wasteful redundancy, because some (maybe all) of the 256 colors are repeated many times over. A better way to store the pixel colors is to set aside 768 bytes in the file for a color palette: 256 entries of 24 bits each identifying the colors used in the image. Then, a pixel color can be represented with an 8-bit value in the range 0 to 255 specifying a color in the color palette. The space required for the graphical portion of the data is now 1,000,768 bytes, down from the 3,000,000 bytes required if a palette is not used. Throw in a few extra bytes for nongraphical data and you've still reduced the file size by almost two-thirds.

Most graphics file formats store pixel values in row-major format. If the image dimensions are 1,000 by 1,000 and each pixel is represented with 8 bits, the first 1,000 bytes of the file's graphical data hold the colors of the pixels in the image's top row (in order of occurrence from left to right), the second 1,000 bytes hold the colors of the pixels in the second row, and so on. Some formats, however, reverse the order of the rows. BMP files, for example, start with the bottom row of pixels and work upward.

Every bitmapped file format structures graphical and nongraphical data differently. Rather than try to generalize further, let's take a close-up look at one file format—the BMP format used extensively in Windows and OS/2. In particular, we'll look at a Windows BMP file describing a 1,000-by-1,000 image with 256 colors. (The BMP format differs slightly depending on whether the image contains a maximum of 2, 16, 256, or 16.7 million colors. The Windows and OS/2 BMP formats also differ just a bit, hence this file's description as a Windows BMP.) The file contains four major parts: a 14-byte file header, a 40-byte information header, a 1,024-byte color table, and 1 million bytes of pixel data, in that order. (The color table consumes 1,024 bytes instead of 768 because BMP files pad each 24-bit color table entry with an extra, unused byte.) We'll also examine the process that a drawing or illustration program might go through to read this file and display the image on the screen.

How BMP Files Are Stored

1 The first 14 bytes of the BMP file constitute the file header. The *file header* contains three pieces of information: a signature consisting of the letters *BM*, which identifies the file as a BMP file; a number indicating the file size; and a number specifying the location within the file where bitmap data begins. The latter value is expressed as a byte count from the beginning of the file. Two other fields in the file header are reserved for future use and normally contain zeros.

2 Pertinent nongraphical data is stashed away in the *information header*. Fields in the information header specify, among other things, the size of the information header (40 bytes in Windows-style BMP files), the image's height and width in pixels, and the number of bits of color information per pixel.

3 The *color table* holds 256 entries of 4 bytes each. The first byte in each entry specifies a color's blue component, the second byte the green component, and the third byte the red component. The fourth byte is unused and is normally set to 0. If the first three values in the color table are 0, 192, and 192, then color number 0 is medium-intensity yellow (a mixture of red and green). The color table defines every color used in the image.

4 The remainder of the file holds bitmap data. Since the image contains 1 million pixels and each pixel requires 8 bits, or 1 byte, of color information, this portion of the file is 1 million bytes in length. The ordering of the bytes reflects the left-to-right order of pixels, starting with the bottom line in the image. Each byte value identifies a color in the color table.

File header

BM signature (2 bytes)
File size (4 bytes)
Reserved (2 bytes)
Reserved (2 bytes)
Location of bitmap data (4 bytes)

Information header

Size of information header (4 bytes)
Image height (4 bytes)
Image width (4 bytes)
Number of color planes (2 bytes)
Number of bits per pixel (2 bytes)
Compression method used (4 bytes)
Number of bytes of bitmap data (4 bytes)
Horizontal screen resolution (4 bytes)
Vertical screen resolution (4 bytes)
Number of colors used in the image (4 bytes)
Number of important colors (4 bytes)

Color table

0	192	192	0
192	0	192	0
192	192	0	0
128	128	128	0
140	244	04	0
		48	0
136	64	32	0
60	255	202	0

Bitmap data

Pixel values for bottom row (1,000 bytes)
Pixel values for second-from-bottom row (1,000 bytes)
Pixel values for third-from-bottom row (1,000 bytes)
...
...
...
...
...
...
...

5 To display an image stored in a BMP file, a program reads the file header and information header. This tells it the dimensions of the image and the number of colors that it contains.

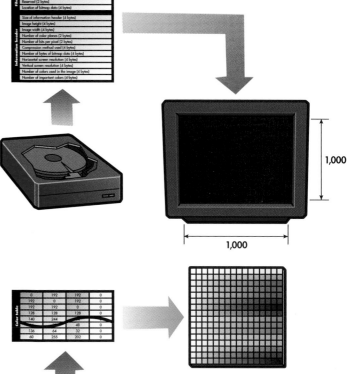

6 The program then reads the color table. If this computer displays a maximum of 256 colors, the software programs the computer's color palette with the values in the color table. This ensures that the colors in the image will be displayed correctly. If the computer can display thousands or perhaps millions of colors, the hardware palette does not have to be programmed.

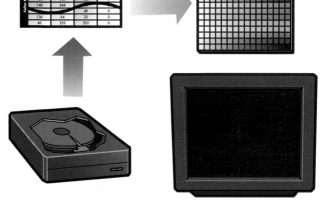

7 Bitmap data is read last. As rows of pixel values are read from the file, they are transferred to the video buffer to produce an image on the screen. In graphical operating environments such as Windows, the program doesn't transfer the values directly; it passes them to Windows, and Windows moves them into the video buffer.

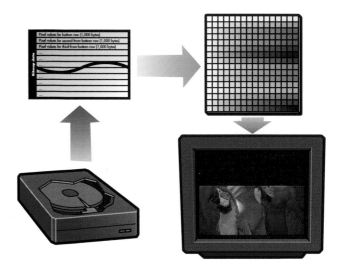

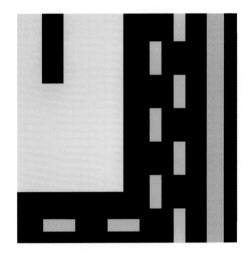

Image Compression

THE PROBLEM WITH bitmapped files is that they can get big—very big. Disregarding the overhead associated with file headers and other nongraphical data, the file size is proportionate to the number of pixels in the image and the number of bits required to represent each pixel. A true-color 1,024-by-768 image contains more than 2 megabytes of pixel information. One second of television-quality video stored in bitmapped form consumes about 30 megabytes. Bitmaps such as these can fill up a hard disk very quickly. Even a compact disc, which holds nearly 700 megabytes of data, is no match for the bitmapped graphics monster unless steps can be taken to reduce the volume of data.

Fortunately, graphics files don't have to take up megabyte after megabyte of disk space. A technique called *image compression* can knock most any graphics file down to size. Image compression methods use clever tricks to reduce the number of bytes needed to represent graphical information. Depending on the compression method used and the contents of the graphics file (some files compress a lot better than others), it's not uncommon to see a large graphics file shrink down by a factor of five or more. Some compression methods deliver even higher savings, but at a cost: Some of the color information is lost when the image is restored to uncompressed form. As a result, the restored image may appear slightly blurred and discolored compared to the original.

The methods used to compress bitmapped file data fall into two broad categories: *lossless compression* and *lossy compression*. Lossless methods yield lower compression ratios but preserve every pixel in the original image. Lossy methods deliver higher compression ratios, but sacrifice the ability to reproduce the original, uncompressed image pixel for pixel. For files created by a CAD or spreadsheet program, it's important to preserve all the information because the loss of one bit could alter the meaning of the entire file. But bitmap data is different. The eye doesn't perceive all the subtle color shifts in a typical bitmapped image, so some of the detail can be discarded without affecting the overall informational content.

In this chapter, we'll look inside two common image compression methods and see how they work. First we'll investigate one form of run-length encoding (RLE), a process that replaces sequences of repeating numbers in a graphics file with two numbers: one that specifies the length of the run (the number of times the value is repeated), and another that specifies the value itself. This is a very common—and very simple—lossless method that is used in one form or another in many of today's popular graphics file formats, including PCX and BMP. It takes advantage of the fact that most graphical images contain redundancies in the form of adjacent pixels of identical values. To picture how RLE compression works, imagine an image with 100 consecutive pixels whose value is 0. Now imagine replacing the 100 zeros with a 100 and a 0. As a consequence, you've compressed this part of the image by a factor of 50.

The second method we'll look at is JPEG (pronounced *jay-peg*), a lossy compression method that takes its name from the organization that developed it: the Joint Photographic Experts Group. JPEG is widely used to compress still images stored on compact disc. It is considerably more complicated than RLE, but it produces correspondingly higher compression ratios—even for images containing little or no redundancy. The idea behind JPEG compression is to segregate the information in an image by level of importance, and then to discard the less important information to reduce the overall quantity of data that must be stored. It does this by transforming a matrix of color values into a matrix of amplitude values corresponding to precise frequencies in the image. (Just as a complicated sound wave can be broken down by mathematics into simple sine waves of various amplitudes and frequencies—sine waves that, when added together, reproduce the original signal—a row or column of pixel data plotted on a graph can be represented with amplitudes and frequencies. This has nothing to do with frequencies of light, but with the shapes of imaginary curves that combine to form graphical plots of pixel values. A complex mathematical formula converts the data from one format to the other.) JPEG compression throws away some of the high-frequency components of the image while retaining the low-frequency components. The eye is less sensitive to high-frequency variations in color, so the basic look of the image is preserved in the low frequencies. When the image is decompressed, the resultant pixel values don't quite match the original ones because of the data that was discarded. But they generally come very close.

One of JPEG's most interesting characteristics is that it allows quality factors to be "dialed in" by the user. High quality factors preserve more of the image's detail but yield lower compression ratios. Low quality factors yield more compression but fuzzier images. Basically, the lower the quality factor, the greater the amount of information that gets discarded. The trick to using JPEG effectively is to strike a balance between compression and image quality. This may require some trial and error, because every image responds to JPEG compression a little differently. Some images can be JPEG-compressed to one-tenth their normal size with little degradation. Others suffer unacceptable losses when compressed by half that amount.

When true-color images are compressed using either method (RLE or JPEG), the red, green, and blue components are compressed separately. If the bitmapped image uses palettized color or simply shades of gray, pixel values can be encoded in one pass.

Here's a close-up look at how RLE and JPEG image compression work.

How RLE Image Compression Works

1 If you were to look closely at a bitmapped image, you would find that it's not unusual for pixels of the same color to appear adjacent to one another. And if you were to start in the upper-left corner of the image and go from left to right examining the pixels on each row, writing down pixel values as you went, you'd find that a typical image contained many runs of repeating numbers. The number of pixel values in a run is called the *run length*.

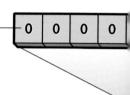

2 Beginning with the image's first row, an RLE compressor scans pixel values from left to right searching for repeating runs. Whenever the compressor finds three or more consecutive pixels of identical value, it replaces them with two values: one specifying the run length, and another specifying the pixels' value. Values specifying run lengths are called *run-length tokens*, and are shown here as triangles.

3 To identify series of nonrepeating pixel values, the compressor inserts tokens (shown here as squares) specifying the number of values that follow. A reserved bit distinguishes tokens specifying run lengths from tokens specifying the lengths of nonrepeating series. For example, a token with 8 bits could specify a series of up to 127 pixels (the highest number you can form with 7 bits) and the eighth bit in each token could be used to specify whether the pixels are repeating or nonrepeating. RLE reduced the size of the scan line in this example from 32 to 19, a savings of 40 percent. This process is repeated for every scan line in the image so that repeating runs are compressed throughout.

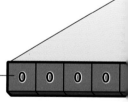

4 A graphics program decompresses the image by reading the compressed file and expanding repeating runs back into the appropriate pixel values. Every bit in every pixel is restored to its original value, so the decompressed image matches the original image exactly.

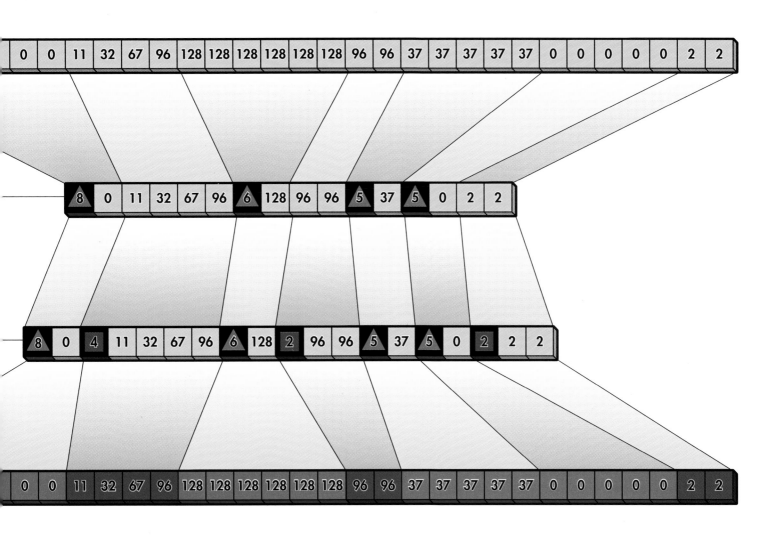

How JPEG Image Compression Works

1 Initially, the compression program divides the image into 8-by-8 blocks of pixel values. Because the time required to compress an image using the JPEG method is a function of the number of pixels in a block squared, processing several smaller blocks of pixels is much faster than processing the entire image at once.

62	65	65	68	72	84	42	18
48	57	60	60	66	66	51	24
45	54	58	60	65	60	48	26
37	48	53	56	53	48	40	33
58	50	52	64	60	51	42	31
64	58	64	72	75	74	49	50
82	72	65	76	76	72	53	38
79	71	60	67	55	58	48	40

2 The pixel values are processed using a formula called a *discrete cosine transform*, or *DCT*. The DCT transforms an 8-by-8 matrix of color values corresponding to different points in the image into an 8-by-8 matrix of amplitude values corresponding to different sine-wave frequencies. Positions near the upper-left corner of the matrix correspond to lower frequencies, and positions near the lower-right corner to higher frequencies.

452	49	-60	34	-7	2	2	-8
-26	-9	-24	4	-19	-4	1	3
32	19	2	16	-8	0	3	-6
23	1	-9	11	5	-2	9	-3
-20	8	7	-4	1	2	0	-5
9	2	-6	3	-1	-4	2	-2
5	-4	-1	-1	0	-3	5	-2
4	10	-2	8	2	4	-3	1

7 Values in the pixel matrix are multiplied by the values in the quantization matrix to reproduce, as closely as possible, the matrix output during the compression process by the DCT. Because of the precision lost in the quantization step, the numbers are close to the originals but do not match them exactly.

453	50	-63	36	-11	0	0	0
-25	-7	-27	0	-13	0	0	0
35	18	0	13	-15	0	0	0
27	0	-13	15	0	0	0	0
-22	13	0	0	0	0	0	0
13	0	0	0	0	0	0	0
0	0	0	0	0	0	0	0
0	19	0	0	0	0	0	0

8 An inverse DCT (IDCT) formula is applied to the matrix to reconstruct the original pixel values. Once again, the numbers do not match the originals because of the information that was lost when the matrix was quantized. The output image will resemble the input image very closely, but some blurring and discoloration will be evident.

60	68	70	69	77	79	49	11
45	55	61	62	68	70	51	26
47	54	59	60	59	54	41	29
40	43	50	57	57	50	40	34
57	53	54	61	63	51	35	24
64	59	59	70	79	74	59	46
81	75	70	72	76	73	58	43
76	72	64	58	59	58	47	34

4 Each value in the matrix output by the DCT is divided by the corresponding value in the quantization matrix and rounded to the nearest integer value. The higher numbers in the lower-right half of the quantization matrix mean that greater portions of the image's high-frequency information will be discarded. The lower-right portion of the pixel matrix now contains mostly zeros.

5 The computer zig-zags through the matrix and uses a combination of lossless encoding methods to compress the data, essentially doing away with zeros in the lower-right half. Lower quality factors produce correspondingly more zeros in the matrix, yielding higher compression ratios.

3 The quality factor input by the user is plugged into a simple formula that generates values for another 8-by-8 matrix called the *quantization matrix*. The lower the quality factor, the higher the magnitude of the numbers in the matrix.

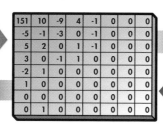

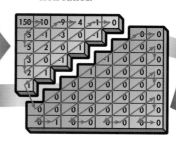

6 To decompress a JPEG image, the computer begins by reversing the effects of the lossless encoding step to reproduce the quantized pixel matrix.

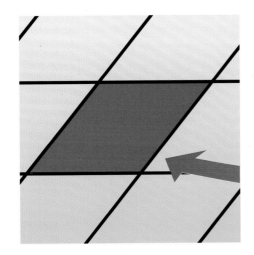

Image Enhancement and Special Effects

THE REAL VALUE in computerized image processing lies in what can be done to an image once it is resident on the computer. Digitally captured photographs can be manipulated in a variety of useful ways. Is the image overexposed? No problem; the exposure is easily reduced by decreasing the color values of the pixels. If desired, red, green, and blue color values can be manipulated separately to achieve better color balance. Is the image out of focus? Blurred images can be sharpened, and crisp, clear pictures can be blurred to mimic the softening effect of photographic filters.

With good image processing software present to lend a hand, there's almost no end to the magic you can do. This chapter examines four image processing effects: blurring, sharpening, embossing, and watercoloring. *Blurring* redistributes the colors in an image in order to soften hard edges, while *sharpening* heightens the differences between the colors of adjacent pixels to bring out hard-to-see details. *Embossing* transforms an image so that figures inside the picture look as if they are embossed on a metal surface, like the profile of George Washington on the face of a quarter. *Watercoloring* converts a photographic image into a watercolor lookalike.

Algorithmically, none of these effects is difficult to achieve. The secret ingredient in each of them is a small matrix of numbers called a *convolution kernel*. A 3-by-3 kernel contains three rows of three coefficients. To transform one pixel in an image, you multiply its color value by the coefficient in the center of the kernel. Then you multiply the eight pixel values surrounding the center pixel by their kernel coefficients, sum all nine products, and assign the resulting value to the center pixel. This process is repeated for every pixel in the image, after which the image is said to be *filtered*. The kernel coefficients determine the outcome of the filtering process. A blurring kernel, for example, consists of a pattern of coefficients, all less than 1, that add up to 1. This means that every pixel will absorb some of the colors of its neighbors, but that the overall brightness of the image will stay the same. (If the sum of the coefficients is greater than 1, brightness will increase; less than 1, and brightness will decrease.) A sharpening kernel contains a center coefficient that is greater than 1, surrounded by negative numbers whose sum is one less than the center coefficient. This magnifies any existing contrast between the color of a pixel and the colors of its neighbors. It sounds a little mystical, but a digital image is, after all, just a bunch of numbers. Massaging the numbers in the right way can produce wondrous—and potentially very useful—effects.

How Blurring and Sharpening Work

1 In preparation for blurring a digitally captured image, the computer reads the image into memory so the red, green, and blue color values of every pixel are known.

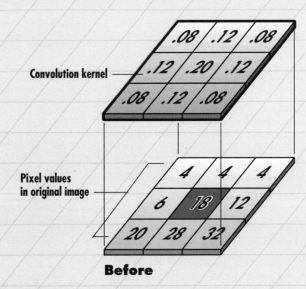

Convolution kernel

Pixel values in original image

Before

2 A 3-by-3 blurring kernel is applied to the red, green, and blue color values of every pixel in the image. The color value for the pixel that lies beneath the center of the kernel is calculated by multiplying the weighting factors in the kernel and the corresponding color values in the image, and summing the results.

4 Sharpening works the same as blurring, except that a different kernel is used. We'll start with the same image as before, but this time the goal is to increase, rather than decrease, the overall clarity of the image.

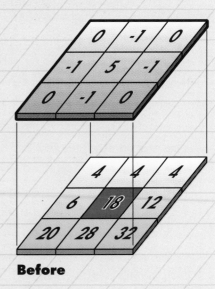

Before

5 Every pixel in the image is processed using a 3-by-3 sharpening kernel. As before, red, green, and blue color values are processed separately and later recombined to form 24-bit color values. The negative weights around the center of the kernel increase the contrast between the target pixel and its neighbors.

$$4 \times .08 = .32$$
$$4 \times .12 = .48$$
$$4 \times .08 = .32$$
$$6 \times .12 = .72$$
$$18 \times .20 = 3.60$$
$$12 \times .12 = 1.44$$
$$20 \times .08 = 1.60$$
$$28 \times .12 = 3.36$$
$$32 \times .08 = 2.56$$
$$\overline{14.40}$$

Modified value for target pixel

14

After

3 The final image appears blurred compared to the original because each pixel's color has been spread among its neighbors. The amount of blurring can be increased by using a larger kernel to distribute colors among a greater number of neighbors, adjusting the kernel coefficients to decrease the coefficient in the center, or filtering the image with a blurring kernel again.

$$4 \times -1 = -4$$
$$6 \times -1 = -6$$
$$18 \times 5 = 90$$
$$12 \times -1 = -12$$
$$28 \times -1 = \underline{-28}$$
$$40$$

40

After

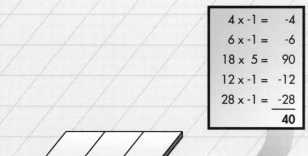

6 The final image is visibly sharper than the original. The extra detail was not manufactured from thin air; the sharpening process simply magnified the existing contrast between pixels. Processing the image a second time may increase the clarity even more.

How Embossing Works

1 Embossing is accomplished in a manner very similar to blurring and sharpening. The process starts with a conventional color image.

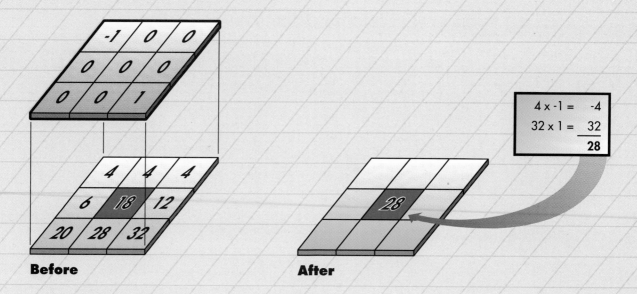

Before

After

$$4 \times -1 = -4$$
$$32 \times 1 = 32$$
$$28$$

2 Every pixel in the image is processed with a 3-by-3 embossing kernel. Unlike the blurring and sharpening kernels, whose coefficients add up to 1, the weights in an embossing kernel add up to 0. This sets the color values of "background" pixels—pixels that do not lie along an edge defined by contrasting colors—to 0, and nonbackground pixels to nonzero values.

3 After a pixel value is processed with the embossing kernel, 128 is added to it. This sets background pixels to medium gray (red=128, green=128, blue=128). Sums that exceed 255 can be rounded down to 255 or "wrapped around" to a value between 0 and 255.

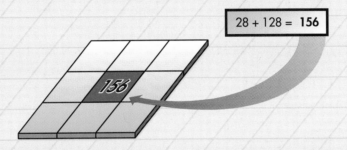

28 + 128 = **156**

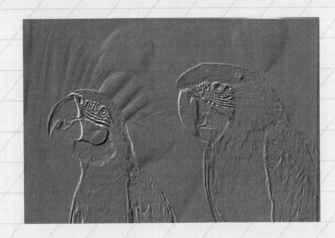

4 In the embossed version of the image, contours seem to rise from the surface. The direction from which the light is cast upon the image can be altered by changing the positions of the 1 and the -1 in the kernel. Swapping these values, for example, would reverse the direction of the light.

How Watercoloring Works

1 A watercolor filter transforms an image so that it looks as if it had been painted with watercolors. Above is a digital image scanned from a photograph.

Before

0	0	4	4	4
0	4	4	4	6
0	6	18	12	12
10	20	28	32	40
12	16	30	16	12

After

		10		

0
0
0
0
4
4
4
4
4
4
6
6
10
12
12
12
12
16
16
18
20
28
30
32
40

◄ Median Value

2 The first step in applying a watercolor filter is to smooth the colors in the image. One way to do this is to perform a median averaging process on every pixel. The color value of each pixel and its 24 neighbors are placed in a list and sorted from lowest to highest. The median (thirteenth) color value in the list is then assigned to the target pixel.

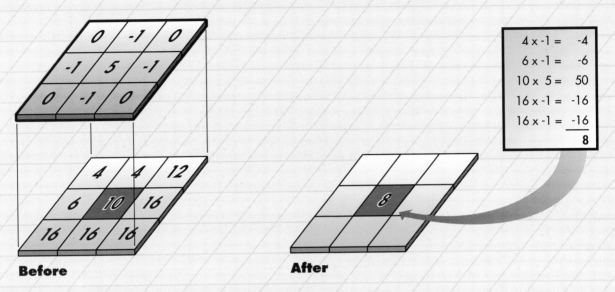

4 x -1 =	-4
6 x -1 =	-6
10 x 5 =	50
16 x -1 =	-16
16 x -1 =	-16
	8

Before

After

3 After smoothing the colors, the computer processes each pixel in the image with a sharpening kernel to make the edges stand out more.

4 The resulting image resembles a watercolor painting. This is just one example of the ways in which unrelated image processing techniques can be combined to produce unusual visual effects.

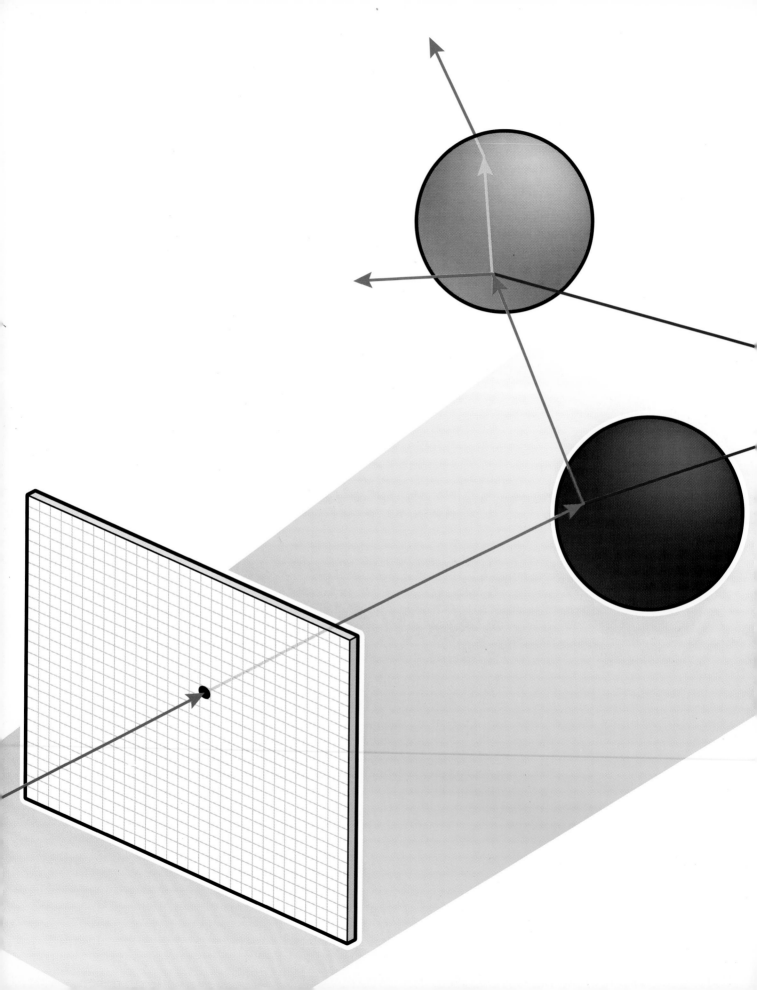

THREE-DIMENSIONAL MODELING AND RENDERING

CONTENTS

Chapter 14: Representing Objects
in Three-Dimensional Space
110

Chapter 15: Viewing Objects in Three-Dimensional
Space: Projections
114

Chapter 16: Shading, Lighting, and Surface Removal
118

Chapter 17: Ray Tracing
128

Chapter 18: Solid Modeling
134

SINCE THE DAWN of the computer graphics age three decades ago, the goal of computer-generated realism—scenes drawn by the computer that are indistinguishable from scenes rendered by nature—has been a holy grail of sorts. All too often, pictures created by a computer *look* as if they were created by a computer. Missing is the infinite variety of detail found in nature: the endless shades of colors, the finely textured surfaces, and the subtle lighting effects.

Researchers are constantly looking for ways to enable computers to produce better-looking images created from mathematical models of objects in the world around us. The images we dealt with in Part 3 weren't created by a computer; they were simply computer replications, scanned from a photograph or input from other sources. *Rendering* is the term computer scientists use to describe the process of generating realistic-looking images from models of real-life (or imaginary) objects. A rendered image is built from the ground up, starting with mathematical descriptions of the objects in the scene. The computer applies color, light, textures, and other effects to make the final product look as much as possible like a photograph. Examples of scenes rendered with astonishing degrees of realism abound in the movie industry. For instance, the stunning metal-man scenes in the 1991 hit *Terminator 2: Judgment Day*, in which the figure of actor Robert Patrick was overlaid with a silvery metal skin, were created on high-powered computer, and were later transferred to film.

Images rendered with such high degrees of realism are often called *photorealistic images*. The calculations involved in producing photorealistic images are both complex and time consuming, often requiring hours or even days of computer time to run. But the ends often justify the means. In time, computers will become fast enough that photorealistic rendering can be done in real time. Thanks to some clever shortcuts that reduce the number of computations involved and the fact that some details can be omitted without compromising the overall quality of the image, it is already possible for some computer systems to produce near photographic-quality images on the fly. There are many applications for this technology, including flight simulators and virtual reality systems.

In Part 4, we'll look at some of the technology involved in modeling three-dimensional objects and rendering them on the computer screen. First we'll look at how three-dimensional models are represented by a computer using a technique known as surface modeling, and how such models are displayed on a two-dimensional screen. Then we'll discuss coloring and lighting considerations and see how surfaces that are obscured by other surfaces are removed from the final image. We'll also take up the subject of ray tracing and touch briefly on texture mapping. The former is a widely used technique for creating incredibly realistic-looking pictures complete with shadows and reflections, and the latter is a technique for overlaying material textures (wood, marble, and so on) onto otherwise featureless surfaces. Finally, we'll discuss solid modeling—an alternative method of representing three-dimensional objects that lends itself to certain scientific uses, such as gauging interference between adjoining parts in close-fitting mechanical assemblies.

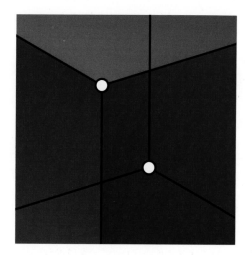

Representing Objects in Three-Dimensional Space

WE LIVE IN a three-dimensional world inhabited by three-dimensional objects. In order for a computer to accurately reproduce these objects, it must be able to represent them in three-dimensional coordinate space.

The conventional way to model real-life objects is to store them as collections of surfaces, a technique known as *surface modeling*. A cube has six flat faces. Each face constitutes one surface, and each is defined by its four corners. It's easy to imagine how a computer might represent this cube: by storing the x, y, and z coordinates of the four corners of each of the six faces. Given a group of four corner coordinates, the computer can draw the corresponding face on the screen. And when all six faces are drawn together, a wireframe image of a cube is formed.

When you hold a solid opaque cube in your hand, you can never see more than three of its surfaces at a time. For the computer to render an accurate image of the cube with hidden surfaces removed, it must be able to identify all six surfaces. If a cube were represented only by the coordinates of its eight corners, the computer would not automatically know how to connect the points to form surfaces. Storing information in the form of surface coordinates rather than discrete, unrelated points allows the computer to show more than just simple wireframes.

Not all objects are as simple to model as a cube. What if an object contains curved surfaces? It's not practical to store the coordinates of millions of points defining a curved surface, because computer memory is a finite resource. There are two ways to avoid this problem. The first is to approximate the curved surface with several smaller surfaces that are flat. The resulting surface is called a *polygon mesh*. The more smaller surfaces (polygons) used, the more accurate the model. The second is to model the curved surface precisely by storing the coordinates of a few representative points that, in conjunction with mathematical equations, can be used to determine the coordinates of other points on the surface. Techniques for doing this abound in the computer graphics world. The *Bézier patch*, which represents a curved or undulating surface with 16 control points, is a popular surface type because it is easily joined with other Bézier (pronounced BAY-zee-ay) patches to form complex surfaces such as those found on the body of an automobile.

Which form of surface representation you use is determined by the software package you're running. Some support flat surfaces only; others support one or more varieties of mathematically precise curved surfaces. Here's a graphical look at both forms of surface representation.

How Objects Are Modeled in Three Dimensions

Some objects can be precisely represented with flat, polygonal surfaces. A cube, for example, can be modeled with six square polygons. The computer stores the x, y, and z coordinates of the four corners of each square. When the edges of the six surfaces are drawn on the computer screen, a wireframe image of a cube is formed.

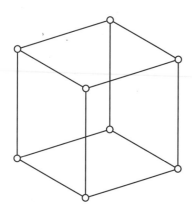

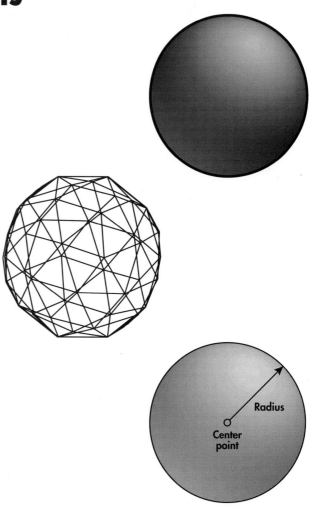

Spherical objects can either be approximated with polygons or represented precisely with the mathematical equation for a sphere. For a polygon mesh model, the computer stores the coordinates of every corner of every polygon. A mathematical model requires only a center point and a radius.

Curved and undulating surfaces can be approximated with polygon meshes or modeled precisely by combining control points with equations that act on the coordinates of the control points. The Bézier patch shown here represents a three-dimensional curved surface with 16 control points, only 4 of which actually lie on the surface (a characteristic of Bézier patches). More complex surfaces can be created by joining together two or more patches.

 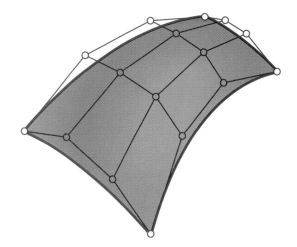

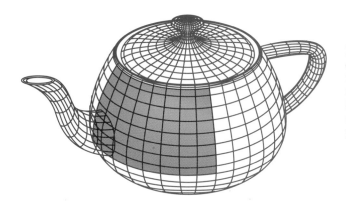

Real-life objects typically contain a variety of curved and flat surfaces. The famous Utah teapot (so called because it was developed by researchers at the University of Utah), shown here with hidden lines removed for clarity, consists of 32 separate Bézier patches. One of the patches on the body of the teapot is highlighted.

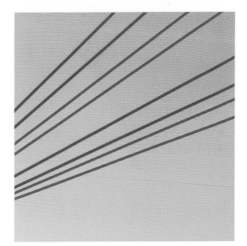

Viewing Objects in Three-Dimensional Space: Projections

ONE OF THE limitations inherent to modeling three-dimensional objects on a computer is that viewing is done on a flat, two-dimensional screen. (Actually, most screens aren't really flat. The vast majority of tube-type screens are curved ever so slightly in one or both directions, but for our purposes it's legitimate to think of them as flat surfaces.) Three-dimensional displays do exist, but for the most part they're still found only in research labs.

To display a three-dimensional object on a two-dimensional screen or other output device, a computer uses a mathematical transformation called a *projection*. Points defining lines, curves, and other entities that make up an object are projected onto a two-dimensional surface, the mathematical equivalent of projecting a movie onto a theater screen. How does it work? An imaginary projection surface called the *viewing plane* is interposed between the observer and the object, perpendicular to the line of sight. Projection lines are drawn from points on the object back to the observer, and the points where the lines intersect the viewing plane identify corresponding points in the projection. For a computer, the locations of these intersections are relatively easy to calculate. And once the points are projected onto the viewing plane, it is a simple matter to transfer the resulting image to the screen. Moreover, different views of the object can be presented simply by changing the observer's position and reprojecting.

Projections fall into two distinct classes: parallel projections and perspective projections. In a *parallel projection*, projection lines are drawn parallel to the observer's line of sight. In a *perspective projection*, projection lines are drawn so that they intersect at the observer's eye. The latter approach creates an effect known as *foreshortening*, in which a feature's projected size decreases as its distance from the viewing plane increases. Perspective projections look more realistic than parallel projections, because objects that are farther away appear smaller, just as they do in real life. Parallel projections are sometimes preferable, however, because they preserve the parallelism between parallel lines in the scene.

Here's a look at both forms of projection, and at the differences in the images that they produce.

How Parallel and Perspective Projections Work

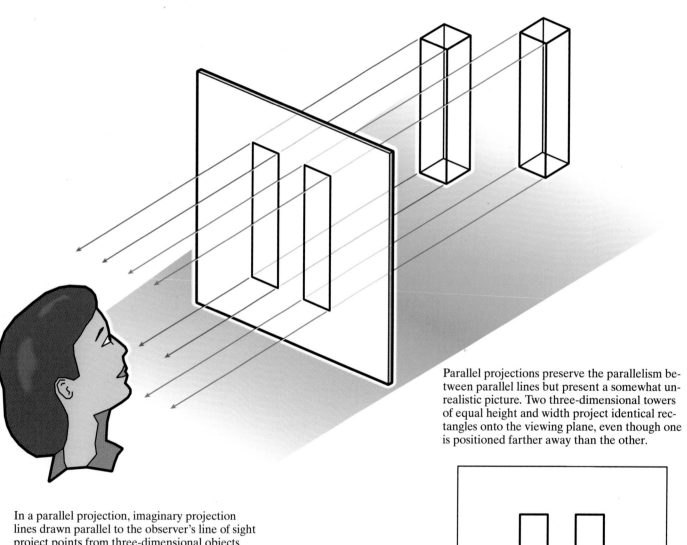

Parallel projections preserve the parallelism between parallel lines but present a somewhat unrealistic picture. Two three-dimensional towers of equal height and width project identical rectangles onto the viewing plane, even though one is positioned farther away than the other.

In a parallel projection, imaginary projection lines drawn parallel to the observer's line of sight project points from three-dimensional objects onto a two-dimensional viewing plane. Plotting points in the viewing plane is a simple matter of calculating where the projection lines intersect the plane.

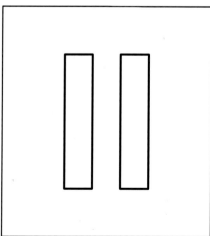

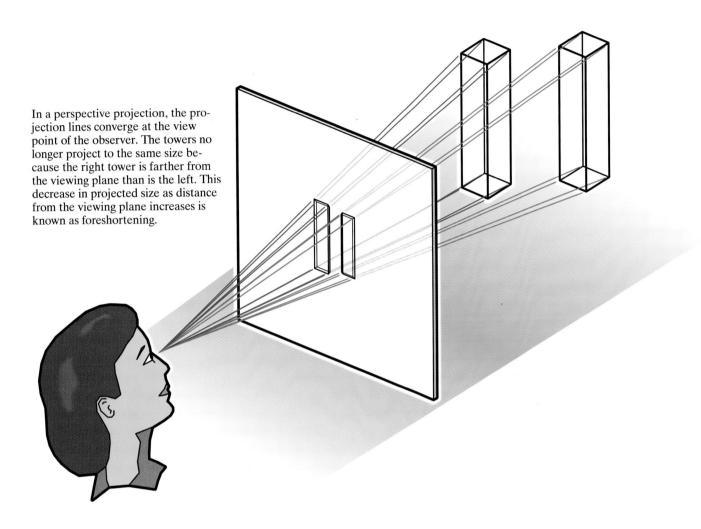

In a perspective projection, the projection lines converge at the view point of the observer. The towers no longer project to the same size because the right tower is farther from the viewing plane than is the left. This decrease in projected size as distance from the viewing plane increases is known as foreshortening.

A perspective view of towers from the same view point as before demonstrates the effect of foreshortening and the added realism that it lends to the scene. All of the towers' faces are visible, and the difference in the projected sizes adds a sense of depth.

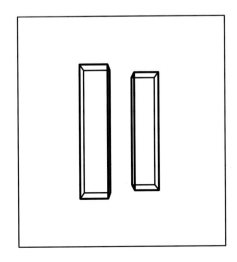

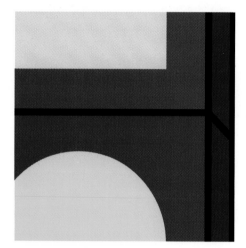

CHAPTER 16

Shading, Lighting, and Surface Removal

WIREFRAME IMAGES ARE easy to produce, but they don't do a very good job of depicting objects as they appear in real life. Most objects have opaque surfaces that obscure other surfaces. No matter what angle you look at them from, some of the surfaces are hidden from view. A wireframe image, by contrast, shows all surfaces, regardless of whether they lie in front of or behind other surfaces.

There are several methods that computer graphics programs may choose from to remove hidden surfaces from an image. One of the simplest and most widely used is a technique known as *z-buffering*. The idea behind z-buffering is simple. As a surface in the model is scan converted into pixel values in the video buffer, the distance from each pixel on the surface to an imaginary reference plane behind the model is calculated also. These distances are recorded in a separate area of memory known as the z-buffer, which contains one entry for every pixel in the image. The computer works through the model, scan converting the surfaces one at a time. If the distance calculated for a given pixel is greater than the distance recorded previously for the same pixel (if, for example, the computer has already scan converted a surface that lies behind the current surface), then the z-buffer is updated with the greater of the two distances and the pixel is assigned the color of the current surface. If, on the other hand, the distance is less than a previously recorded distance (indicating that this point on the surface lies behind a surface that was scan converted earlier), then the z-buffer entry retains its old value and the pixel retains its original color. When all the surfaces have been scan converted, the video buffer holds an image of the model with hidden surfaces removed. One of the advantages of the z-buffer algorithm is that surfaces do not have to be scan converted in any particular order. No matter what the order, the outcome is the same.

Surface removal is but one factor in the many-faceted visual realism equation. Another consideration is to paint visible surfaces with the appropriate colors. The simplest approach is to assign each surface a color and paint it accordingly. However, images rendered this way leave much to be desired. In a real-life image, identically colored surfaces are shaded differently due to the different amounts of light incident upon them. This is most evident when an object is illuminated from the side in a dark room with a bright, directed light source such as a flashlight. Surfaces facing toward the light are brightly illuminated, while surfaces facing away from the light are dark, even black. To produce truly realistic images, a computer must apply shading algorithms to simulate the effects of uneven lighting.

Performing shading calculations amounts to computing the color of every pixel on every surface in the model and varying the colors to account for uneven lighting effects. Techniques for doing this abound, particularly where polygonal models are concerned. We'll look at two of them: flat shading and Gouraud shading. In *flat shading*, each polygon is assigned a hypothetical color. Given a description of an imaginary light source that illuminates objects in the scene, the computer assigns shades of color based on the angle of incident light. The more a polygon faces the light source, the brighter it appears. Every pixel on a given polygon is assigned the same shade, but different polygons are distinguished by different shades. *Gouraud shading* (named after its creator, Henry Gouraud), does flat shading one better by varying the shade of color at different points on a polygon. This produces a more realistic-looking image and makes polygonal models representing curved surfaces look more like smooth-surface models.

By themselves, neither of these shading techniques account for some of the more complex real-life lighting effects such as shadows and specular reflection. (A common example of specular reflection is the dot you see on an apple when you shine a bright light on it. The shiny surface of the apple acts as a mirror, reflecting the light that strikes it.) Other, more advanced shading and lighting algorithms allow effects such as specular reflection, but require commensurately more computer time to run. In general, the more realistic the image, the more work a computer must do to produce it. For many applications, techniques such as flat and Gouraud shading strike a reasonable balance between image quality and the time required to create the image. Here's a peek under the hood at how these two forms of shading work, and how hidden surfaces are removed by z-buffering.

How Z-Buffering Works

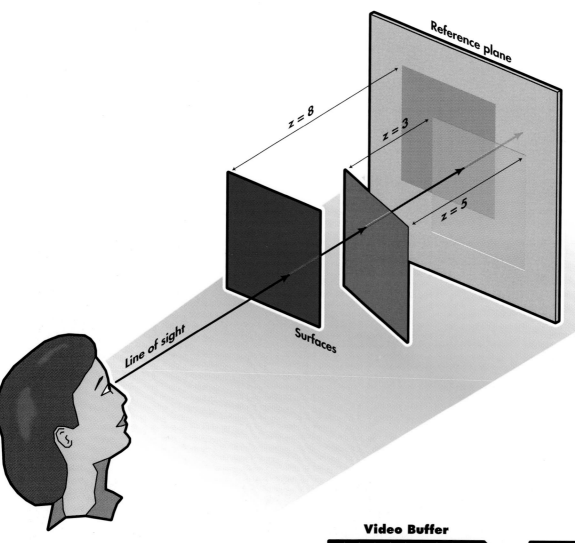

1 Z-buffering allows a computer to remove hidden surfaces by performing simple depth calculations as each surface in the model is scan converted into pixels. At the outset, all values in the video buffer are set to the scene's background color and all values in the z-buffer are set to 0. The z-buffer contains one entry for every pixel in the image.

2 As the blue square is scan converted into pixels, a z-value—the distance from the corresponding point on the surface of the square to an imaginary reference plane located behind the model—is calculated for each pixel. If the pixel's z-value is greater than the z-value stored at the corresponding location in the z-buffer, the new pixel value is copied to the video buffer and its z-value is copied to the z-buffer. Since the z-buffer was initialized to 0 and this is the first surface to be scan converted, a complete image of the blue square is assembled in the video buffer.

Video Buffer

Z-Buffer

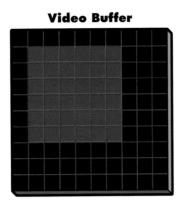

3 When the red square is scan converted, the z-values for pixels that lie behind the blue square are less than the z-values recorded in the previous step. Therefore, only the red pixels that are unobscured by the blue square are copied to the video buffer. The results would have been the same if the red square had been scan converted first, because the blue pixels, with their higher z-values, would have replaced the red pixels.

Video Buffer

Z-Buffer

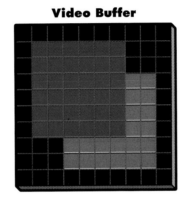

4 These two images, generated from a three-dimensional model of three pushpins, illustrate the result of z-buffering. The image on the left shows a wireframe view of the model. The image on the right is an unshaded version of the same model with hidden surfaces removed.

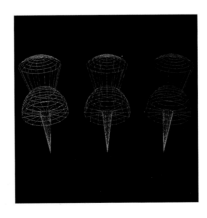
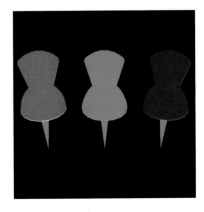

How Flat Shading Works

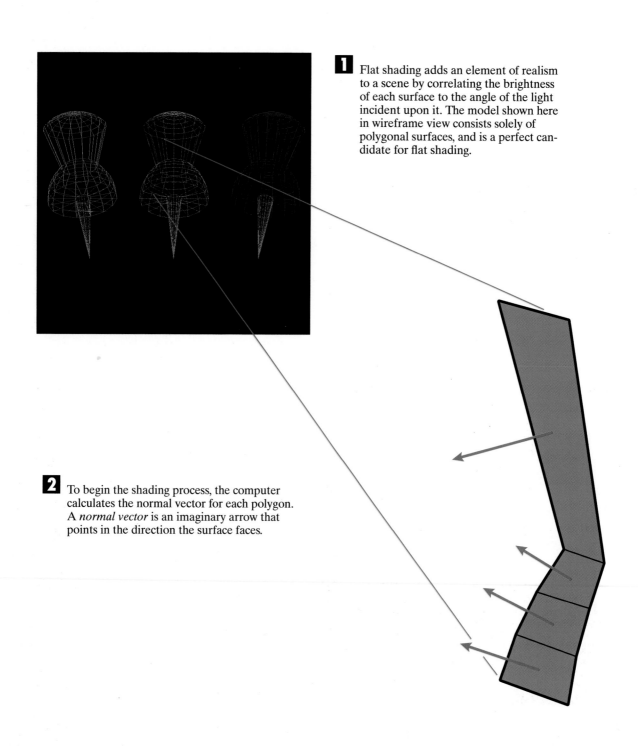

1 Flat shading adds an element of realism to a scene by correlating the brightness of each surface to the angle of the light incident upon it. The model shown here in wireframe view consists solely of polygonal surfaces, and is a perfect candidate for flat shading.

2 To begin the shading process, the computer calculates the normal vector for each polygon. A *normal vector* is an imaginary arrow that points in the direction the surface faces.

Incoming light

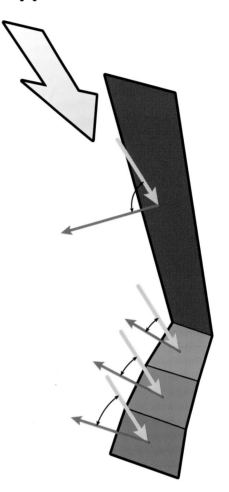

3 Next, the computer calculates the angle between each polygon's normal vector and the direction of light entering the scene from an imaginary light source. Polygons whose normal vectors lie parallel to the direction of light (surfaces that face the light source head on) receive the highest color intensity, while polygons whose normal vectors form angles of 90 degrees or more with the direction of light (surfaces that cannot "see" the light source) are painted black. Mathematically speaking, a surface's brightness is proportional to the cosine of the angle. If you took high school trigonometry, you might remember that the cosine of 0 degrees is 1.0 and the cosine of 90 degrees is 0.0. Therefore, a surface only receives full intensity if its normal vector forms an angle of 0 degrees with the direction from which light enters the screen.

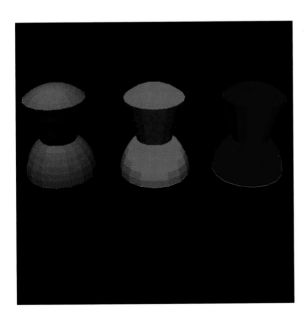

4 The shading process is repeated for every polygon in the image, and a z-buffer or other hidden surface algorithm is applied to hide polygons (or portions of polygons) that are obscured by other polygons. The result is a flat-shaded image.

How Gouraud Shading Works

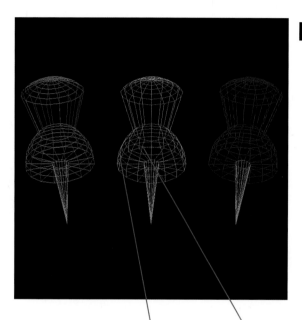

1 Unlike flat shading, which paints all points on a given polygon the same color, Gouraud shading varies the intensity of light—and therefore the color of individual pixels—across a polygon's surface. Here again is a simple polygonal model.

Incoming light

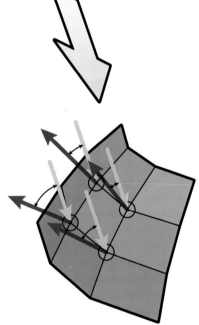

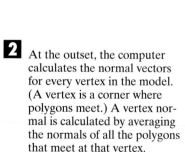

2 At the outset, the computer calculates the normal vectors for every vertex in the model. (A vertex is a corner where polygons meet.) A vertex normal is calculated by averaging the normals of all the polygons that meet at that vertex.

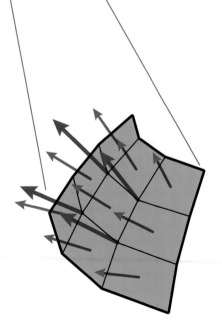

3 For a given polygon, the intensity of light at each corner is calculated in the same way that intensity is calculated for an entire surface when flat shading is performed. The intensity at a vertex is proportional to the cosine of the angle formed by the vertex normal and the direction of incoming light.

4 Colors on the edges and interior of the polygon are interpolated from the colors at the corners. This varies the brightness of different points on the surface and lends an added degree of realism.

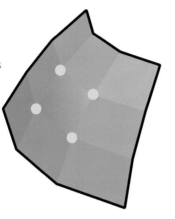

128	131	134	137	140
119	123	127	131	135
111	116	120	125	130
102	108	113	119	125
94	100	107	113	120

5 Processing every polygon in this manner and removing hidden surfaces produces a Gouraud-shaded image. Shading is smoother than in a flat-shaded image because the lines where polygons meet blend together. The only visible evidence that this image was generated from a polygonal model is the rounded edges' slightly angular silhouettes.

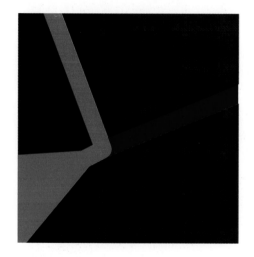

Ray Tracing

SHADING TECHNIQUES SUCH as those discussed in the previous chapter go a long way toward allowing computers to generate lifelike pictures, but they fall short of achieving true photorealism. Real objects cast shadows when they are illuminated by bright lights, and most objects reflect some of the light that hits them. The reflected light, in turn, may go on to illuminate other objects or other surfaces on the same object. And some objects are wholly or partially transparent, permitting a portion of the light that hits them to pass through and possibly go on to illuminate still other objects. Computer scientists have terms to describe these phenomena: shadowing, reflection, and transmission. A rendering program must take all of these phenomena into account if it is to produce genuinely photorealistic images.

The interplay between these various lighting effects is complex. A single surface in a scene may be illuminated by light from several different sources. Fortunately, techniques exist that allow computers to take all these forms of lighting into account. The best known is *ray tracing*, which was originally developed as a means for hidden surface removal and later extended to include the effects of shadowing, reflection, and transmission. Ray tracing isn't the final word in photorealistic rendering (it, too, has its weaknesses, and is often combined with other rendering techniques to further refine three-dimensional images), but it's close enough that it can be used to produce stunning images that are near photographic in quality. The greatest drawback to ray tracing is that it is slow. Even a supercomputer may require hours to render a complex scene from start to finish. The same operation could require days on a PC.

Ray tracing is complex mathematically but simple conceptually. What the computer is really doing is tracing rays of light from the light sources to the eye. Tracing backward rather than forward, from the eye to the light sources instead of from the light sources to the eye, increases the efficiency of the process by ensuring that the number of rays reaching the eye will be exactly the same as the number of pixels in the image. To picture the process, think of your monitor screen as a window through which you can see a three-dimensional model drawn by your computer. Imaginary lines called *rays* are drawn from your eye through each pixel on the screen and projected into the model. Each time a ray strikes a point on a surface, additional rays are spawned. If the surface is reflective, a *reflected ray* is generated. If the surface is transmissive, a *transmitted ray* is generated, taking into account the fact that light bends as it passes from one medium to another, a phenomenon known as refraction. Some surfaces are both reflective and transmissive, spawning both kinds of rays. The paths of these rays are traced throughout the model, and if they strike other surfaces, still more rays are spawned. At every point where a light ray strikes a surface, a *shadow ray* is drawn from the point of intersection to each light source in the scene. If a shadow ray strikes another surface before it reaches the light source, the surface that it was drawn from is shadowed by the surface that blocks its view of the light. Mathematically, all these rays, together with data describing the physical characteristics of the objects in the model (color, tranparency, shininess, and so on), tell the computer the color and intensity of every pixel in the image.

One of the deficiencies of standard ray tracing is that ray-traced surfaces do not have textures like real surfaces. They're smooth—sometimes too smooth. To compensate, ray tracing programs frequently use *texture mapping* or *bump mapping* techniques to add textures to surfaces in the model. Texture mapping "paints" a bitmapped image—of wood, for example, or marble—onto a surface. Bump mapping takes advantage of the fact that ray tracing, like other forms of shading, uses surface normal vectors in its calculations. Bump mapping perturbs an object's surface normal vectors according to a predefined pattern (the bump map), transforming a smooth surface so that it looks rough and nonuniform.

To help you picture how ray tracing works, the following illustration traces the path of a single ray from the eye through a pixel on the screen, and the paths of the rays that it spawns.

How Ray Tracing Works

2 A reflected ray is fired from the first ray's point of intersection with the sphere. The surface is opaque, so no transmitted rays are spawned. A shadow ray traces the path from the point of intersection to the light source. Since the shadow ray doesn't intersect another opaque object, the light source will make a direct contribution to the intensity of the pixel.

1 To backward-trace all the light that makes a contribution to one pixel on the screen, the computer fires an imaginary ray from the observer's eye through the pixel and traces it until it hits an object.

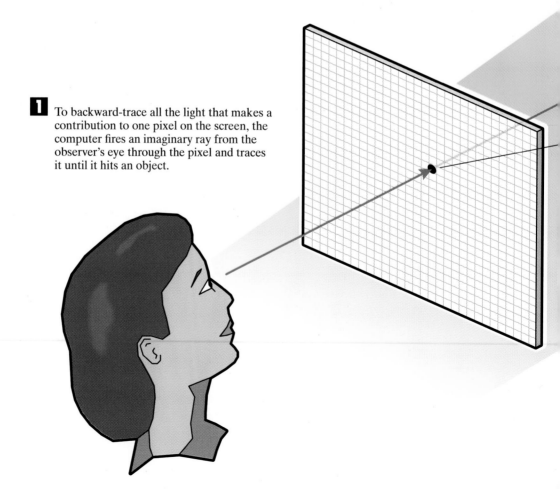

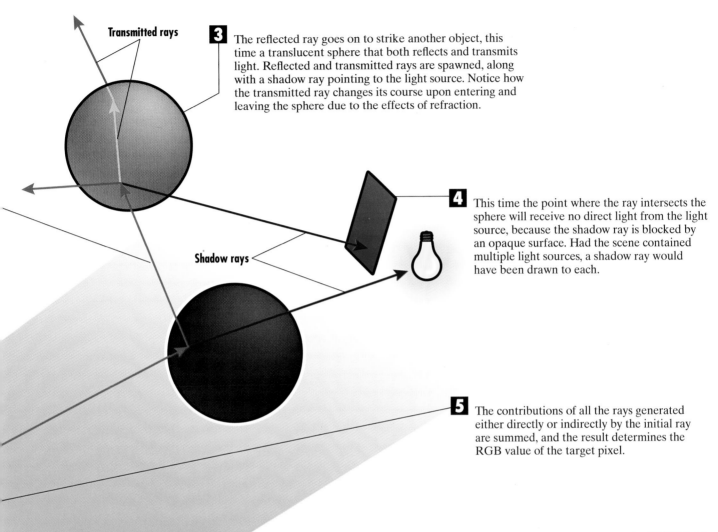

Transmitted rays

Shadow rays

3 The reflected ray goes on to strike another object, this time a translucent sphere that both reflects and transmits light. Reflected and transmitted rays are spawned, along with a shadow ray pointing to the light source. Notice how the transmitted ray changes its course upon entering and leaving the sphere due to the effects of refraction.

4 This time the point where the ray intersects the sphere will receive no direct light from the light source, because the shadow ray is blocked by an opaque surface. Had the scene contained multiple light sources, a shadow ray would have been drawn to each.

5 The contributions of all the rays generated either directly or indirectly by the initial ray are summed, and the result determines the RGB value of the target pixel.

6 This is a ray-traced scene rendered in 30 minutes on a 50 MHz 486DX-based computer using Polyray, a popular shareware ray-tracing program. The sphere in the left foreground has a mirrored surface. The middle sphere has a shiny opaque surface, and the sphere on the right is composed entirely of glass. Note the reflections exhibited on several of the surfaces, the refracted image of the gold sphere in the glass sphere, and the shadows cast by the two light sources. Also note that perspective projection and hidden surface removal are natural consequences of the ray tracing process, and do not require special consideration.

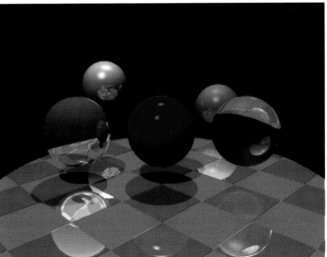

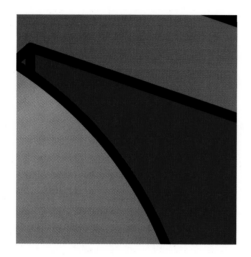

Solid Modeling

SURFACE MODELS ARE keen for making pictures, but they fall short when it comes to examining properties other than outward appearance. What happens when you cut a sphere in half? If it's a real, solid sphere, you get half a sphere that is also solid on the inside. If it's a surface-model sphere, you get something entirely different: a hollow, bowl-shaped object. The surface model looks solid from the outside, but a simple cutting operation exposes the truth: Surface models don't model the whole object. They model only the skin.

Solid modeling is a branch of computer science that addresses these deficiencies by modeling objects as mathematical solids rather than as hollow shells. The two forms of modeling are closely related. One popular form of solid modeling, in fact, uses surfaces to define an object's shape. But solid modeling extends the modeling paradigm to encompass the notion of mass; to recognize that the molecules of matter inside an object are different from the air outside it. This may sound like an abstract distinction, but it is critical to certain applications. Solid models can be used to calculate the weights and centers of gravity of irregularly shaped objects, to predict the outcome of machining operations in which material is removed from an object, and to gauge interferences between mating parts in an assembly, among other things. None of this is impossible with surface models, but solid models are infinitely better suited to the task.

There are many forms of solid modeling. The most prevalent is the *constructive solid geometry* method, better known as CSG. CSG uses Boolean set operations to build representations of solids from the unions, intersections, and differences of simpler solids known as *primitives*. Using CSG, a cube with a hole in it might be modeled by subtracting a cylinder—a primitive representing the hole—from a cube. By itself, a cube with a hole is difficult to represent mathematically. But cubes and cylinders are easy to represent, and by extension a cube with a hole is easy to represent if it is represented in terms of its primitives.

CSG models are stored in hierarchical structures called trees. Each fork in a tree points to two solids that are combined with a Boolean set operation to form a more complex solid. The more complex the object, the more branches and primitives there are. If you start at the bottom of the tree and work your way up, combining primitives as you go, you end up with the final model. Here's a graphical look at Boolean set operations and the CSG modeling method.

How Boolean Set Operations Work

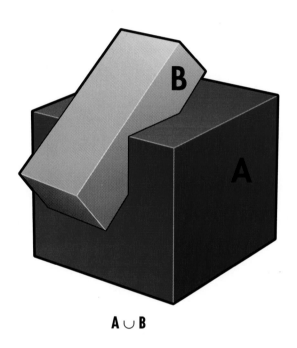

A ∪ B

1 Many forms of solid modeling, including the CSG method, rely on Boolean set operations to build complex solids from simpler, more easily defined solids such as cubes, cylinders, and spheres. This unconventionally shaped object, which would be difficult to represent as a single mathematical entity, is formed by combining a cube (A) and a brick-shaped object (B). The resultant object represents the union of the two primitives, signified with a ∪ symbol.

2 The intersection of the two primitives yields an entirely different object: a triangle-shaped wedge. Intersections are denoted with a ∩ symbol.

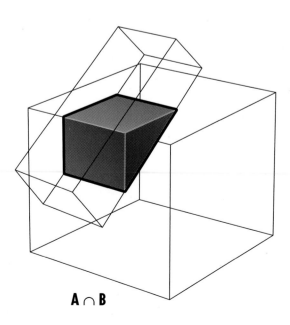

A ∩ B

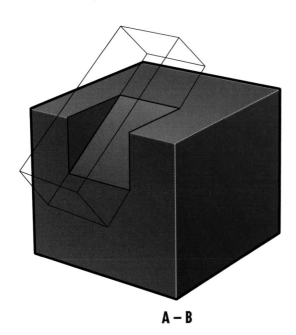

A – B

3 Taking the difference between the two primitives—in this case, subtracting the brick from the cube—yields a cube with a slot cut in it. Once again, this object would be difficult to represent mathematically. But it's easy to represent when it's defined with a Boolean set operation involving two primitives.

4 Subtracting the cube from the brick rather than the brick from the cube yields yet another solid, this time a rectangular object with a V-shaped groove in it.

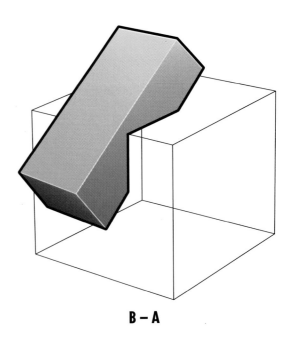

B – A

How Constructive Solid Geometry Works

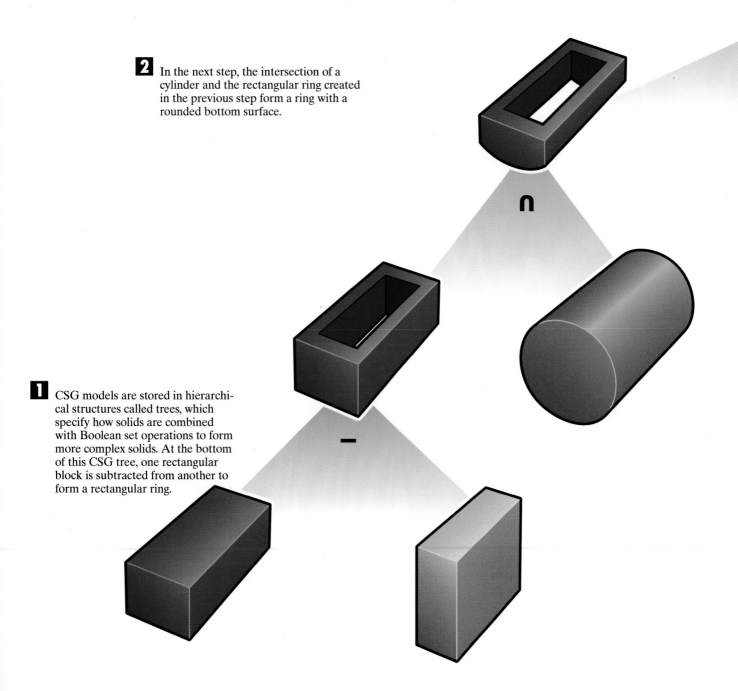

2 In the next step, the intersection of a cylinder and the rectangular ring created in the previous step form a ring with a rounded bottom surface.

1 CSG models are stored in hierarchical structures called trees, which specify how solids are combined with Boolean set operations to form more complex solids. At the bottom of this CSG tree, one rectangular block is subtracted from another to form a rectangular ring.

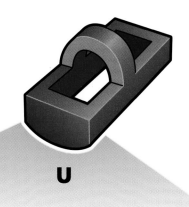

U

5 The union of the rectangular ring from the left half of the tree and the arch from the right half forms a solid model of this object, which defies easy mathematical definition using conventional methods. To display the model on the computer screen, a solid modeling program would recreate the geometry by traversing the tree from bottom to top, and then scan convert the visible surfaces of the solid primitives.

4 Subtracting a rectangular block from the ring creates an arch.

3 In the lowermost branches of the right half of the tree, a small cylinder is subtracted from a larger cylinder to form a circular ring.

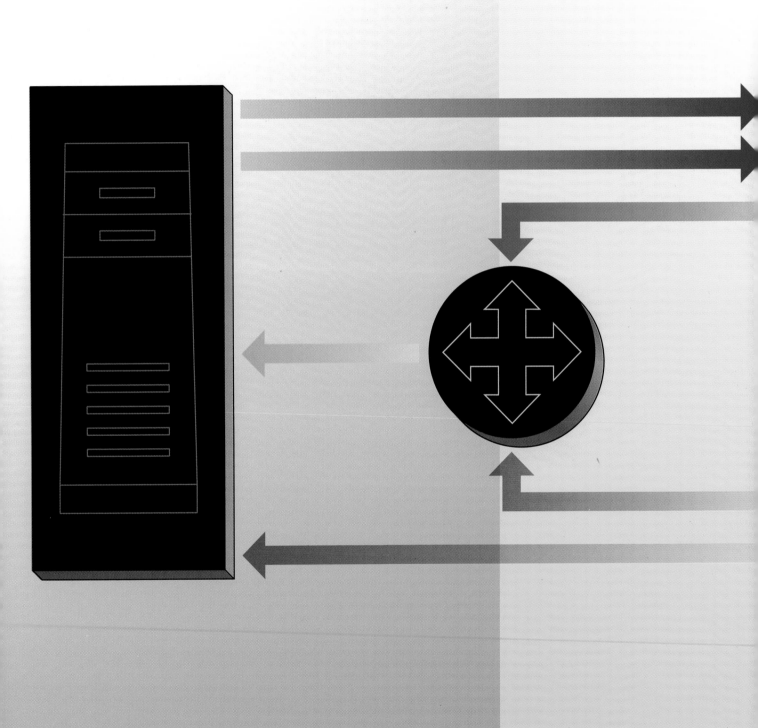

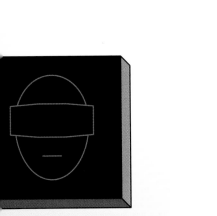

FINAL FRONTIERS

CONTENTS

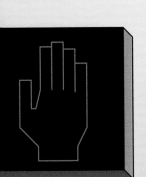

Chapter 19: Computer Animation
144

Chapter 20: Fractals
152

Chapter 21: Morphing
162

Chapter 22: Virtual Reality
168

OVERVIEW

COMPUTERS GAINED A foothold in our culture because they are powerful number crunchers. The first computers were little more than sophisticated electronic adding machines that could perform millions of mathematical calculations in the time a person could perform only a few. In this capacity, computers played crucial roles in many of America's major post-World War II technical achievements, from automating large-scale business transactions to building better nuclear weapons to landing astronauts on the moon.

It wasn't until much later, in the 1960s, that computers began to take on a new dimension: as tools for simulating the world in which we live with pictures. Over time, computer graphics evolved from crude line drawings into beautifully textured images equal to anything an artist could create by hand. Today, the science of computer graphics is concerned with more than pretty pictures. While research continues to advance the state of the art in fields such as image processing and three-dimensional modeling and rendering, much of the leading-edge work is focused on bringing computer graphics to life. Recent advances in video compression and decompression techniques, for example, enable computers to store and replay vast quantities of bitmapped data in real time, producing animation whose quality equals and sometimes exceeds that of television. Three-dimensional displays utilizing laser holograms or images projected onto spinning mirrors will soon permit physicians to view computer-generated models of organs and tissues as if the real thing were sitting on a bench in front of them. Virtual reality systems block out the real world and enclose the user in an imaginary universe where the normal rules of physics need not apply. Even lowly video games push the envelope, incorporating the latest in sound and animation techniques to create new worlds on your desktop. In the future, computers will be used not only to simulate our world, but to shape new worlds and new dimensions that exist only in the imagination.

In the fifth and final part of *How Computer Graphics Work*, we'll explore some of the more exotic applications for computer graphics and the key technologies that underlie them. First, we'll look at animation techniques that enable computers to display moving pictures. Then we'll journey into the fractal dimension, where abstract mathematical concepts of infinity are brought to life in beautiful swirls of color. Next we'll look at morphing, which enables moviemakers to depict stunning shape changes involving real-world objects. Finally, we'll take up the subject of virtual reality: what it is, how it works, what kinds of hardware and software are involved, and how the computer fools your mind into seeing something that's not really there. All in all, it's a fitting close for a trip through the multidimensional space known as computer graphics, and for a book that endeavors to bring the occupants of that space to life.

Computer Animation

STILL IMAGES ARE fine for some computer graphics applications, but others call for moving images. Flight simulators and video games, for example, continuously change the screen to make objects, and even entire scenes, appear to move. Rapidly changing the image on the screen to create the illusion of motion is called *animation*.

All computer animation is achieved in basically the same way: by making incremental changes to the screen image rapidly enough so that a sequence of images appears to be a moving picture. Science tells us that it takes about one quarter of a second for the human brain to see and comprehend a picture. When you watch a film in a movie theater, you see 24 different images, or *frames*, every second. Each frame is displayed for about $\frac{1}{24}$ of a second. Your mind doesn't perceive individual frames; it perceives a moving picture. Computer animation works the same way. Most of today's personal computers are incapable of displaying 24 full-screen images per second, but acceptable animation can be achieved with substantially fewer. The trick is to fit in as many frames as possible and to minimize the latency between frames (the time it takes to draw a new image on the screen). If the person using the computer can see new frames being drawn, the overall effect is greatly diminished.

The best computer animation is produced by *double buffering*, a technique that is also known by the names *screen swapping* and *page flipping*. Double buffering reduces interframe latency to the absolute minimum possible—to the $\frac{1}{60}$ of a second or so that it takes for a monitor's sweeping electron beams to complete one pass over the screen. A program that employs double buffering maintains two video buffers, only one of which is displayed at any given time. All drawing takes place in the background video buffer, which is hidden from view. When a new image is completed in the background buffer, the program flips a switch that swaps the buffers, bringing the background buffer to the foreground and pushing the other to the background. When the switch occurs, the new image appears almost instantaneously. No matter how long it takes for the computer to generate each new screen image, the person using the program sees only the end result, and changes flow smoothly from one frame to the next.

One of the first programs to use double buffering on the IBM PC was the Microsoft Flight Simulator. If you own a copy, start it up and notice how fast the screen updates are—not the number of frames per second, which tends to be fairly low, but the imperceptible latency between frames. New images aren't drawn onto the screen; they just appear. The slight pause between frames is due to the time required to draw a complete new screen image in the background.

Not all video adapters support double buffering. And even if the video adapter supports double buffering, the operating system may not. If only a small part of the scene changes from frame to frame—for example, if the background stays the same while an object moves in the foreground—then an alternative approach is to redraw just the portion of the screen that changes, and to do it too quickly for the eye to see. This process of alternately drawing and erasing a bitmapped image in different locations is sometimes called *block animation*. Typically, a program will copy a rectangular chunk of the background to an off-screen memory buffer. The object is drawn into the rectangle, and when it's time for the object to move to a new location, erasure is accomplished by copying the background rectangle back to the video buffer. The erasing part of the process is easy, but unless the object is also shaped like a rectangle, drawing it requires some ingenuity. Bitmaps are always rectangular, and copying a rectangular bitmap to the screen produces, naturally enough, a rectangular image. If the object is not rectangular, the leftover areas of the rectangle must somehow be encoded so that their pixels are "transparent," retaining their background color even after the bitmap is applied.

Masking is a commonly used technique for drawing an irregularly shaped object on the computer screen without disturbing the background. The object is described with two rectangular arrays of numbers: an AND mask and an XOR mask. The AND mask blacks out those pixels that correspond to the object, leaving the rest unchanged. The XOR mask draws the object in the pixels blacked out by the AND mask, again leaving the background unchanged. Applying the AND mask followed by the XOR mask draws the object on the screen without disturbing the pixels surrounding it. In effect, the AND and XOR masks enable the computer to distinguish between pixels on and off the object in a rectangular area of the screen.

Though it lacks an official name, the combination of block animation and masking is often referred to as *mask animation*. By repeatedly copying the background underlying an object to an off-screen memory buffer, drawing the object on the screen with the AND and XOR masks, and erasing it by restoring the background, a program can achieve animation. Mask animation is used in many video games. The quality of the animation depends to a large degree upon how fast the object can be erased and re-drawn. The smaller the region of the screen that is being updated and the faster the computer, the better the overall effect.

There are other styles of computer animation. On palette-based video adapters, for example, a lava flow can be simulated quite effectively by reprogramming the palette between frames. This method is very fast, because reprogramming one palette register (a RAM-like hardware location whose contents determine the color associated with a single palette entry) changes the color of every corresponding pixel on the screen in the blink of an eye. Palette animation is interesting, but its uses are limited, and it's likely to become an increasing rarity as more and more graphics adapters move away from palettes in favor of 24-bit color. We will therefore concentrate on under-standing the two more prevalent forms of animation: double buffering and mask animation.

How Double Buffering Works

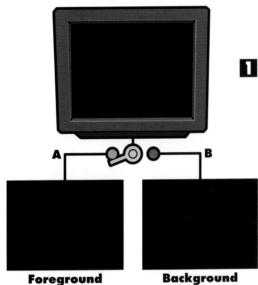

1 A computer graphics application that employs double buffering maintains two separate video buffers, which we'll refer to as buffers A and B. A switch on the video adapter determines which video buffer is shown on the screen. The buffer that the switch points to is referred to as the foreground buffer, and the other as the background buffer. The switch can be toggled back and forth with software commands, effectively swapping the foreground and background buffers and quickly changing what appears on the screen. Initially, both video buffers are empty and the switch points to buffer A.

2 To begin the animation sequence, the computer draws an image into buffer B. The drawing process is hidden from view because buffer B is not displayed.

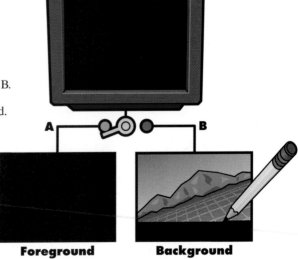

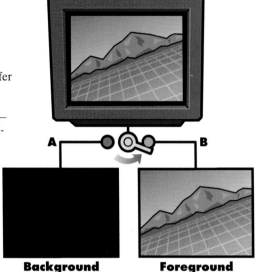

3 Toggling the switch swaps the buffers, bringing buffer B to the foreground and displaying the image that was just drawn. When the switch occurs, the new foreground image appears almost instantaneously—in the $\frac{1}{60}$ of a second or so that it takes for the monitor to refresh the screen.

Background   **Foreground**

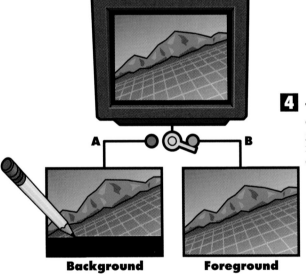

Background   **Foreground**

4 The second scene in the animation sequence is drawn into buffer A, which is now the background buffer. Once again, the drawing action is hidden from view because the screen shows only what's in the foreground.

5 Swapping the buffers a second time displays the second screen in the animation sequence. This process—drawing an image in the background buffer and swapping the buffers—is repeated over and over to create a moving image. No matter how long it takes for the computer to create each new screen, all the user sees is the completed images. However, the higher the frame rate (the more quickly the screens can be drawn and displayed) and the smaller the incremental difference between frames, the smoother the animation.

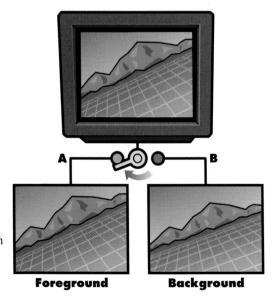

Foreground   **Background**

How Mask Animation Works

1 Mask animation is frequently used when a small, nonrectangular object is moved about the scene against a backdrop formed by a full-screen image. A pair of masks stored in main computer memory serves as a template for drawing the object. The AND mask, which stamps a silhouette of the object into a background image, outlines the object with 0s in a field of 1s. The XOR mask, which draws the object in the impression created by the AND mask, contains the pixel values depicting the object. In this example, 4 represents the color red and 6 represents yellow. Background pixels are represented by 0s.

Object

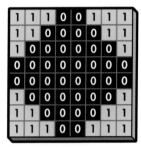

AND Mask

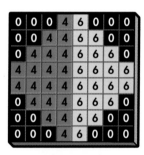

XOR Mask

2 At the outset, the background scene is drawn into the video buffer.

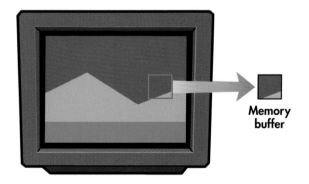

Memory buffer

3 A rectangular block of pixels at the location where the object will first appear is copied from the video buffer to a small buffer set aside in main computer memory.

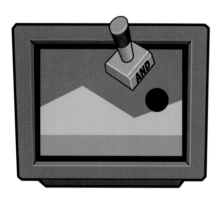

4 The AND mask is applied to the same rectangular region of the video buffer. Pixels that correspond to 1s in the AND mask remain unchanged, while pixels that correspond to 0s are set to 0. The object is now silhouetted against the background.

5 The XOR mask is applied at the same location. Pixels that correspond to 0s in the XOR mask remain unchanged; other pixels assume the color values specified in the mask. The object is now fully displayed on the screen.

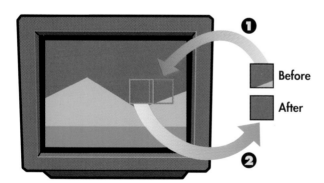

Before

After

6 To animate the object's movement, the computer first erases the object by copying the background rectangle back to the video buffer. Then it makes a copy of the background underlying the object's new location.

7 The object is drawn in its new position with the AND and XOR masks. If it is repeatedly erased and redrawn in this manner and the steps are performed quickly enough, the object will appear to glide across the screen.

CHAPTER
20
Fractals

OF ALL THE DIFFERENT pictures that a computer can create, few rival fractal images when it comes to sheer beauty. For most of us, the word *fractal* conjures up visions of swirling patches of color forming intricate, detailed patterns. But the term actually has a much broader context. A fractal is an object that possesses infinite complexity, exhibiting just as much detail when viewed up close as it does when viewed from afar. The earth is a classic example of a fractal object. Seen from space, it looks like a ball. As you zoom in, it grows in detail to reveal oceans, continents, coastlines, and mountain ranges. Zoom in on a mountain range and still more detail becomes evident; a single plot of ground on the surface of the mountain is, at its own scale, as complex and undulating as the mountain itself. An even closer look reveals tiny grains of dirt that are themselves fractal objects.

Computers enable us to build models of such infinitely detailed structures. There are many methods for creating fractals on a computer. A pair of mathematics professors at Georgia Tech developed a widely used technique called *Iterated Function Systems* (IFS), which produces realistic-looking images of natural objects such as ferns and trees by repeatedly applying transformations that move, scale, or rotate portions of the image. IFS exploits the self-similarity evident in many products of nature by modeling an object as a composite of many smaller copies of itself. Fractal images with multicolored whorls are generally examples of *escape-time* fractals, which plot points in the complex plane with colors reflecting the length of time required for each point's orbit to go beyond ("escape") a specified boundary. The *complex plane* is like a graph with an x and a y axis. Given a pair of coordinates, a point can be plotted in the complex plane like a point on a graph. But numbers in the complex plane have a rather unusual quality: They possess an imaginary component called i that is equal to the square root of –1. (That's why i is *imaginary*—in reality, the square root of –1 does not exist.) This distorts the normal rules of mathematics so that conventional operations such as multiplying two numbers yield very unconventional results.

The most famous fractal of all, the Mandelbrot set, is an escape-time fractal. For each point on the screen, the computer calculates the coordinates of a series of points defining an imaginary path called an orbit. Points whose orbits never escape an imaginary cylinder centered about the origin of the complex plane are said to be members of the Mandelbrot set, and are tra-ditionally colored black. Points whose orbits *do* escape the cylinder are colored accord-ing to how quickly they escape. A pixel whose orbit escapes the cylinder on the sixth point, for example, might be colored blue, while one whose orbit requires seven points to escape might be colored red. The resulting image depicts the Mandelbrot set and its surroundings, with "unstable" regions of the fractal—regions where a slight change in location produces a dramatic difference in orbital behavior—characterized by dense patterns of color. Changing the formula used to calculate the orbits produces other, equally exotic escape-time fractals.

The infinitely detailed structure of the Mandelbrot set becomes evident when you zoom in at any arbitrary location. No matter how small a region you examine, the pic-ture you see is equally complex. Why? Because in a two-dimensional plane like the one that the Mandelbrot set is plotted in, any area contains an infinite number of points. When you pick a region for display, the computer correlates pixels on the screen to points in the region. And every point, no matter how close it is to its neigh-bor, has a characteristic orbit producing characteristic patterns of color.

Fractals are not merely mathematical curiosities; they have genuine—and use-ful—applications in the real world. Fractal landscapes, for example, have been used as backdrops in science fiction movies, most notably in *Star Trek II: The Wrath of Khan*. IFS fractals are used for image compression, often delivering many times the compres-sion ratios of JPEG and other lossy compression methods with little sacrifice in image quality. Escape-time fractals are used to model the behavior of chaotical dynamic sys-tems (systems in which a minute change in an input condition produces large changes in the output) such as weather patterns.

Enough talk. Let's look at some fractals and the infinite variety of patterns con-tained therein. In order to enrich your understanding of the fractal creation process, we'll also step through the IFS algorithm used to draw a fern and the escape-time algorithm that brings the Mandelbrot set to life.

How the Mandelbrot Set Is Drawn

1 The Mandelbrot set is the most famous fractal in the world. It is also a classic example of an escape-time fractal. Points making up the Mandelbrot set are plotted in an imaginary place called the complex plane, which is similar to a graph with an x and a y axis. But whereas a conventional x-y graph plots real numbers, the complex plane plots complex numbers—numbers with real and imaginary components. This turns the normal rules of mathematics upside down and sets the stage for some very unconventional results.

2 For each pixel on the screen, the computer performs a series of calculations involving the corresponding point in the complex plane. The point's coordinates are plugged into a simple equation that yields a new pair of coordinates. These coordinates are plugged into the same equation again, and yet another pair of coordinates is generated. Repeating this process numerous—typically several hundred—times produces a set of coordinates defining an imaginary path called an orbit. Though the orbit lies entirely within the complex plane (it has two dimensions, not three), it is pictured here rising above the plane as an aid in visualization.

3 If a point's orbit never escapes a cylinder of a particular diameter drawn about the origin of the complex plane, the point is said to be a member of the Mandelbrot set. Points that fit this criterion are normally colored black.

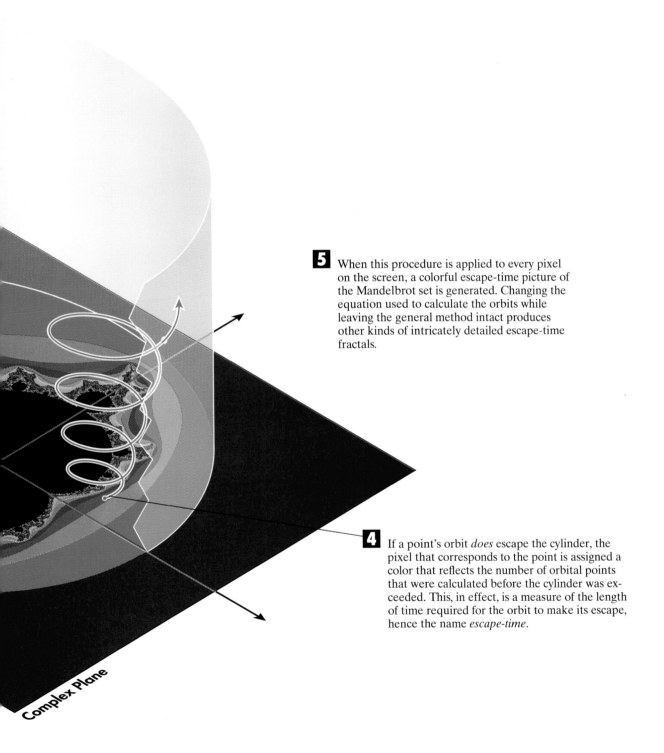

Complex Plane

5 When this procedure is applied to every pixel
on the screen, a colorful escape-time picture of
the Mandelbrot set is generated. Changing the
equation used to calculate the orbits while
leaving the general method intact produces
other kinds of intricately detailed escape-time
fractals.

4 If a point's orbit *does* escape the cylinder, the
pixel that corresponds to the point is assigned a
color that reflects the number of orbital points
that were calculated before the cylinder was ex-
ceeded. This, in effect, is a measure of the length
of time required for the orbit to make its escape,
hence the name *escape-time*.

The Infinitely Detailed Nature of Fractals

1 When you magnify a conventional image, pixels on the screen get blown up, producing a closer but no more detailed view. A fractal image, however, expands to reveal additional detail. This colorful picture of the Mandelbrot set depicts points that are members of the Mandelbrot set—points whose orbits stay within the cylinder—in black, and points whose orbits escape in an assortment of colors. Each pixel in the image represents one point in fractal space.

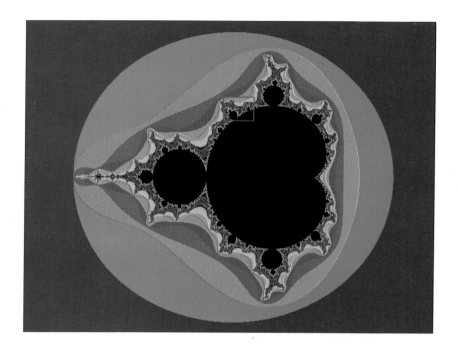

2 Zooming in on the region outlined with a rectangle in the previous image reveals more about the fractal's structure. Each pixel still represents one point in fractal space. But since the screen is now covering a smaller area, the theoretical points are closer together. Note the similarity between the bays in the fractal coastline and the larger lake-like image of the Mandelbrot set. This phenomenon, which is known as *self-similarity*, is characteristic of many fractals.

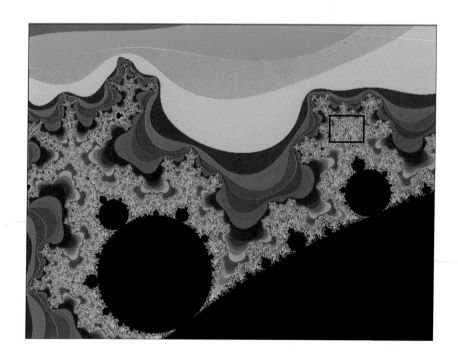

3 Zooming in again reveals still more detail. No matter how far you zoom in, you'll never reach the end of the Mandelbrot set. Details will continue to appear forever.

4 The colors used to signify different orbits are selected at the viewer's discretion. Often, changing the color scheme casts an entirely different light on the subject. Here's another view of the region pictured in the previous image, with colors altered to emphasize the crystal-like structures in this region of the fractal.

How IFS Fractals Work

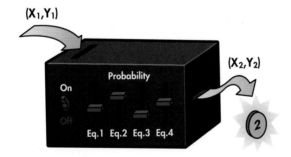

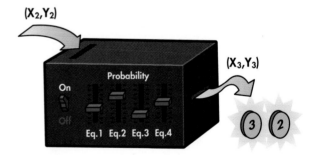

1 A perfect example of an IFS fractal is a computer-generated image of a fern. A crucial element in the creation of the fern is a black box containing a set of four equations known as *affine maps*. Initially, the screen is cleared and the x-y coordinates of a seed point are input to the black box. One of the equations is selected at random (guided by a set of probabilities that determines how often, on average, each equation will be used), and that equation produces a new coordinate pair. Afterward, the screen pixel at those coordinates is illuminated.

2 The coordinate pair generated in the previous step is fed back into the black box. Once more, a randomly chosen equation produces a new coordinate pair, and the corresponding pixel on the screen is lit. This process is repeated thousands of times. Gradually, a screen image begins to coalesce from the randomly scattered pixels.

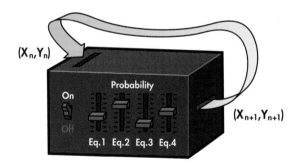

(X_n, Y_n)

(X_{n+1}, Y_{n+1})

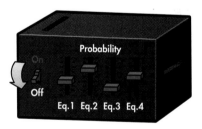

3 As the iterative coordinate-generation process continues, the pixels slowly but surely take the shape of a fern. The varying brightnesses of the individual pixels is due to the fact that some pixels are "landed on" more than once. The more times a pixel's coordinates come out of the black box, the brighter that pixel is colored.

4 The final image is a remarkably accurate depiction of a real-life fern. Note the self-similarity evident in the fern's structure: Each frond is a scaled-down image of the fern itself. Fractal image compression works on the same principle. The compression program searches for self-similarities in the image and derives a set of equations that, when iterated, reproduce the original image as closely as possible. Decompression is then a simple matter of picking a seed value and iterating until the image reaches an acceptable quality level.

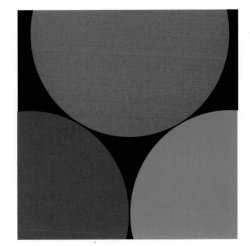

CHAPTER 21

Morphing

ONE OF THE hottest and most talked about effects in computer graphics these days is *morphing*—the production of animated sequences in which an object changes shape or transforms into a different object altogether. The term *morph* comes from the word *metamorphosis*, which means a physical change in form or structure. Morphing as we know it today has been seen in everything from music videos to television commercials to movies. It was a movie, in fact, that made morphing a household word. In one of the most famous scenes ever projected onto the big screen, a blob of liquid metal shaped itself into the figure of actor Robert Patrick in 1991's *Terminator 2: Judgment Day*. Morphing was one of several computer graphics technologies involved in this seemingly supernatural transformation.

Commercial morphs such as these are laboriously rendered frame by frame on expensive computer graphics workstations. Animators at Industrial Light & Magic (ILM), the San Rafael, California–based company that pioneered the art of movie morphing and other special effects, spent several thousand hours creating the effects for *Terminator 2*. Most of the work was done on multiple-processor Silicon Graphics 300-series workstations with up to 64 megabytes of RAM each. ILM built three-dimensional wireframe computer models depicting key stages of the metamorphosis, using as the final model an electronic replica of Patrick himself. Custom software aided in creating the in-between wireframes and adding a reflective metal skin. The resulting images were then digitally composited onto (combined with) background scenes filmed with real cameras, producing a startling sequence that looked as if it were real.

An earlier and equally stunning morph depicting a moving car turning into a running tiger was produced for Exxon Corporation by Los Angeles–based Pacific Data Images (PDI). The car and tiger were filmed separately against blue backgrounds and transformed into *mattes*—clean images of the subjects minus any backdrops. The frames were transferred to digital video tape and then into a computer, and elements of each were meticulously combined to simulate a flowing transition starting at the nose of the car and proceeding toward the rear. Finally, the frames were composited with a background of desert footage shot from a moving vehicle, and the resulting commercial provided an entertaining break for television viewers nationwide.

Recent software developments have made morphing a much easier and less time-consuming pursuit. Given a pair of images to serve as "before" and "after" and a set of control points correlating features in the two, a number of inexpensive morphing packages will generate the in-between images for you. Played back at several frames per second, these images depict a smooth transformation from one state to the other. If the control points are chosen properly, the animation can be quite convincing.

Fundamentally, this type of morphing is a blend of two simple yet interesting computer graphics techniques: warping and cross-dissolving. *Warping* exerts unseen forces at precise points in the image, stretching and shrinking it like a reflection in a funhouse mirror. Algorithmically, warping is accomplished by dividing an image into polygon-shaped pieces like a jigsaw puzzle and distorting the polygons by moving their vertices. Knowing the before and after coordinates of each of the polygons' vertices, the computer can determine the polygons' intermediate shapes through simple interpolation. *Cross-dissolving* is a technique for smoothly shifting from one color to another. For a single pixel, cross-dissolving is accomplished by incrementally changing the pixel's red, green, and blue values. If the colors of the pixels within the polygons are cross-dissolved as the polygons themselves are warped, the result is a morph. It might look complicated, but for a computer it's very simple—as the pictures on the next page illustrate.

How Morphing Works

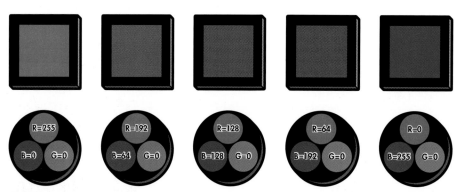

1 Cross-dissolving is accomplished by fading out the pixels of one image while fading in the pixels of another. In this example, a red square is dissolved to blue by incrementally decreasing the red component of each pixel while increasing the blue component.

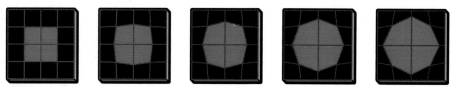

2 One way to warp an image is to divide it into pieces like a jigsaw puzzle (a process known as *tesselation*) and mathematically transform the individual polygons. Once the starting and ending coordinates of a polygon's vertices are known, intermediate coordinates can be computed through simple interpolation. Therefore, it's a trivial matter for the computer to generate in-between images depicting intermediate stages of the tesselated image. Here, a square is warped into a circle in five iterations.

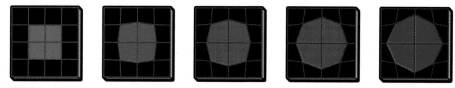

3 Morphing is a combination of warping and cross-dissolving. The sequence of frames shown on the right is identical to the sequence shown above, except that the colors of the pixels inside the polygons change, too. The resulting animation shows a red square morphing into a blue circle. The more frames there are and the more rapidly they are displayed, the smoother the transformation appears.

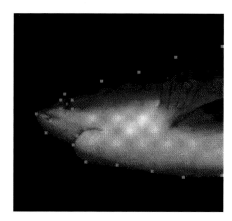

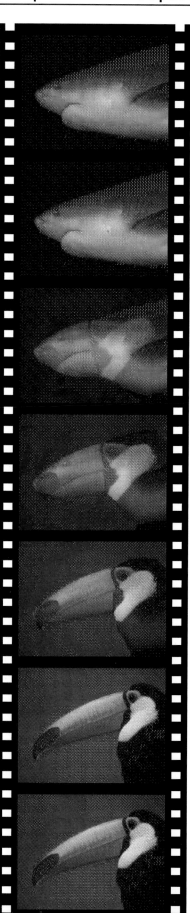

4 Most morphing programs start with a pair of images—one depicting the initial scene and the other depicting the final scene. The person using the software creates control points in one of the images and the computer duplicates them in the other. These points guide the tesselation process. By realigning the control points in either of the images, the user can control the warping and thus the flow of the pixels during the transformation. Here, points in a picture of a shark have been mapped by the user to corresponding points in a picture of a toucan.

5 The frames to the right were created from the images shown above with North Coast Software's PhotoMorph, a popular PC-based morphing program that runs under Microsoft Windows. Notice how the shark's mouth grows into the more elongated mouth of the toucan by virtue of the control points linking the two together. Correlating features of the starting and ending images in this manner produces a more realistic morph.

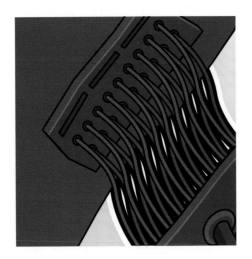

Virtual Reality

MAGINE A COMPUTER environment in which there are no keyboards and mice; where images aren't displayed in front of you, but all around you; where moving your head up, down, or to the side allows you to look around at your simulated surroundings; where you can reach out and touch the objects drawn by the computer; and where gestures such as pointing a finger or opening and closing a hand are interpreted as computer commands—in short, an environment that blocks out the physical world and replaces it with the silicon-fired imagination of a computer. This is virtual reality at its best: a computer-generated universe in which you, the user, step through the looking glass and become a part of the world inside the computer.

Virtual reality has been a dream of computer scientists for decades, but it is only in recent years that computers have become fast enough, hardware compact enough, and graphics sophisticated enough to make that dream a reality. The term *virtual reality* was coined by Jaron Lanier, founder of VPL Research and one of the early pioneers in the effort to make virtual reality commercially viable. Virtual reality is an artificial reality created by a computer that is so enveloping that it becomes the reality perceived by your mind. Have you ever become so involved in a video game that you were no longer aware of what was going on around you? Think how much more absorbed you would become if you could step into the computer and become part of the game and its environment; if looking over your shoulder you saw enemy players instead of the door to your office. That's the essence of virtual reality.

Virtual reality exists today in many forms. A flight simulator that encloses a pilot in a simulated cockpit showing computer-generated views of the world outside the plane is a virtual reality system of sorts. A more traditional virtual reality setup uses headsets and data gloves. The headset serves as your eyes and ears to the virtual world, projecting sights and sounds generated by the computer. The data glove is a virtual extension of your arm, allowing the computer to translate hand and finger movements into actions in the simulated environment. Sensors inside the headset and glove continuously transmit information regarding the position and orientation of your head and hand, enabling the computer to tell where you are looking, reaching, or pointing.

How might such a system be used? Picture a scene with a ball sitting on a table. Pointing a gloved finger in the direction of the table moves you toward the table. With the gloved hand, you reach for the ball. In the headset, you see a computer representation of your own hand reaching out and picking up the ball. When you let go, the ball falls to the floor, producing an audible noise. Pivot your head down and you see the ball resting on the floor. This scenario demonstrates two of the key criteria for virtual reality systems: one, that the system *immerses* you in its world so completely that you feel like you're in it; and two, that the environment is *interactive*, responding to and allowing itself to be modified by your actions. You might become totally absorbed in a video game you're playing on your computer, but it doesn't strictly qualify as a virtual-reality experience because if you look away from the monitor, the physical world swings back into view. Similarly, a movie projected onto a 360-degree screen may seem frighteningly realistic, but because it lacks interactivity, it doesn't truly constitute virtual reality.

Virtual reality will one day enable us to build the ultimate video game, but the real interest in virtual reality stems from its potential to benefit humanity. Virtual reality will someday permit us to take virtual walks on the surfaces of distant planets; voyage through the blood vessels of the human body; join molecules with our hands; train doctors to perform complicated surgeries; walk through homes before they are built; and much, much more. The potential is so vast that there will undoubtedly be applications that we've yet to conceive of. Virtual reality is the most demanding application for computer graphics there is, requiring hardware and software capable of supporting real-time, interactive, three-dimensional graphics. Once the reaches of this frontier are explored, one can only wonder what challenges will rise to confront us next.

How Virtual Reality Works

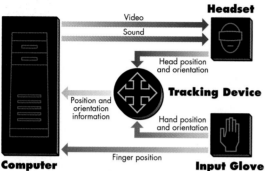

Video → **Headset**
Sound →

Head position and orientation

Tracking Device

Position and orientation information

Hand position and orientation

Finger position

Computer   **Input Glove**

1 Virtual reality hardware comes in many flavors, but a typical system consists of a computer, which stores a description of a simulated three-dimensional world in a database; a headset, which projects sights and sounds created by the computer; a glovelike input device that allows the user to manipulate objects in the virtual world and send commands to the computer; and an electromagnetic tracking device, which monitors the position and orientation of small sensors mounted on the headset and glove.

2 The headset displays images of the virtual world on a pair of small LCD screens similar to the one on a Sony Watchman. Positioned just two to three inches from the viewer's eye, each screen shows a slightly different view of the simulated world (just as you see slightly different views of the real world in your left and right eyes) to lend depth to the scene. Special lenses may be used to expand the field of view to enhance the effect on the peripheral vision, and to converge the images so the headset doesn't act like an ill-fitting pair of binoculars. To reduce graininess due to the low resolutions of most LCD screens, many headsets use diffusion filters to blur the images ever so slightly and tiny pixel-like meshes to make the images appear more detailed than they really are. Some high-resolution headsets used by the military display images on tiny CRT screens mounted above each ear. Mirrored optics reflect the images into the viewer's eyes. In the future, head-mounted lasers may project images directly onto the retina.

3 Earphones built into the headset transmit sounds generated by the computer. Your brain identifies the direction a sound comes from by measuring slight variations in the volumes and arrival times of sound waves reaching your left and right ears. Sophisticated virtual reality systems mimic these auditory effects to add spatial qualities to the sounds that they produce. Virtual reality researchers call this *three-dimensional sound*.

4 The tracking device transmits low-frequency signals, which induce small voltages in coils inside the headset sensor. When the head moves, the voltage levels change. The tracking device feeds this information to the computer, which redraws the images projected into the headset to reflect the head's new position and orientation. This enables a user to "look around" a virtual world simply by moving his head. The tracking device and computer must be able to process information very quickly to avoid bothersome lag times—delays between the time the head is moved and the image is updated in the headset.

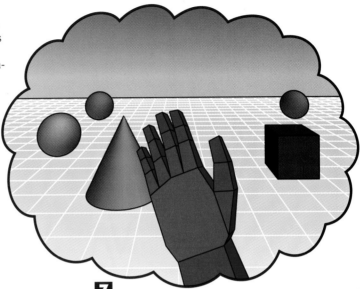

7 To the user, who sees and hears only what is projected into the headset, the virtual world created by the computer supplants the physical world. Here, the traveler journeys through a three-dimensional world populated with objects that may be picked up and moved. In the future, virtual-reality systems will be used in a wide variety of scientific, medical, entertainment, and domestic applications.

6 Sensors in the glove communicate the positions of the fingers to the computer. Tiny fiber optic cables running to each joint loop back to light-sensitive photodetectors. Bending a joint reduces the amount of light passing through the cable. Simple commands may be transmitted to the computer by hand signals. A closed fist, for example, might mean "pick up the nearest object," while an extended index finger might mean "move me in that direction." Researchers are experimenting with gloves that provide tactile feedback, but such devices are still years away.

5 A sensor attached to the glove transmits information about the hand's position and orientation. When the hand wearing the glove is moved or turned, a virtual hand depicted in the headset moves and turns also, enabling the user to reach for objects in the virtual environment.

A

ADCs (analog-to-digital converters), 81, 83

Adobe Photoshop, 75

Adobe Type Manager, 66

affine maps in IFS fractals, 160

aircraft flight simulators, 5–6, 8–9

Aldus PhotoStyler, 75

algorithms

    antialiasing scan conversion, 69, 70

    with convolution kernels for digital image
        enhancement, 99, 100, 102

    described, 33

    for determining best-fit colors, 42

    for dithering, 36

    hidden surface, 8, 119

    line-adjacency boundary fill, 52, 58–59

    midpoint circle, 51, 56–57

    midpoint line, 51, 54–55, 69

    for warping (morphing technique), 164

    z-buffer, 119, 122–123

analog-to-digital converters (ADCs), 81, 83

animation, 143, 145–151

antialiasing, 69–71

ASCII numbering system for characters, 65

associative dimensions, 15

Atari, 25

B

best-fit algorithms, 42

Bézier patches, 111, 113

bitmapped files, 85–86, 88–89

bitmapped fonts, 61, 64–65

bitmaps, 61

block animation, 146

blurring of digital images, 99, 100–101

Boolean sets, 135, 136–137

boundary fills of shapes in pixels, 52, 58–59

bump mapping, 130

Bushnell, Nolan, 25

C

CAD, 11–12, 14–15

cameras, digital, 77, 78, 80–81

CAT scans (computerized axial tomography),
    17, 20–21

CCDs (charge-coupled devices), 77

CDs (compact discs) and CD-ROM drives, 25,
    77

cels, 25

character cells, 65

charge-coupled devices (CCDs), 77

circles, drawing with midpoint circle
    algorithm, 51, 56–57

collimators in CAT scanning, 20

color error, 42, 43

color optimization of palettes, 45

color palettes

    and color optimization, 45

    described, 36

    information to DACs, 38

and median-cut color quantization, 45–46, 48–49

selection in dithering process, 42

colors

in cross-dissolving (morphing technique), 164, 166

digital camera and scanner handling of, 78

displaying via pixels, 32, 35–39

in dithered images, 41, 42–43

in fractal images, 159

in lighting effects, 15, 119–120, 127

in magnetic resonance imaging (MRI), 22

trade-off with resolution, 36, 40–41

in typical video games, 28

color table for .BMP files, 88

complex planes in fractals, 153

compressing bitmapped image files, 91

JPEG (Joint Photographic Experts Group) technique, 92–93, 96–97

RLE (run-length encoding) technique, 91–92, 94–95

computer-aided design (CAD), 11–12, 14–15

computer graphics. *See also* colors; fonts; pixels

animation, 145–147

color representation, 35–37, 45–46

described, 3

drawing and filling shapes, 51–52

examples of applications, 3, 108

image enhancement, 99

image input, 77–78

image modeling, rendering and projections, 111, 115, 135

image storage, 85–86, 91–93

image surfaces and lighting effects, 119–120, 129–130

smoothing jagged lines (antialiasing), 69

text and fonts, 61–62

computerized axial tomography (CAT or CT), 17, 20–21

constructive solid geometry (CSG) method of solid modeling, 135, 136, 138–139

convolution kernels for digital image enhancement, 99, 100, 102

coordinates. *See also* images in three dimensions

in computer-aided design, 14, 15

in median-cut color quantization, 46, 48–49

in midpoint line or circle algorithms, 51, 54–57

in video games, 28, 29

cross-dissolving (morphing technique), 164, 166–167

CSG (constructive solid geometry) method of solid modeling, 135, 136, 138–139

cubes, 111, 112

curves, 14, 112

D

DACs (digital-to-analog converters), 38

DCTs (discrete cosine transforms), 97

diffusion dithering, 36, 41, 42, 45

digital cameras, 77, 78, 80–81

digital signal processor (DSP), 81

digital-to-analog converters (DACs), 38

digitizing tables, 14

dimensions in CAD images, 15

direction vectors, 29

discrete cosine transforms (DCTs), 97

dithering

　　described, 36, 41

　　diffusion technique, 36, 41, 42, 45

　　pattern technique, 36, 41

dot pitch of monitors, 39

double buffering for animation effects, 145, 148–149

downloadable fonts, 64

DRAM (dynamic RAM) for image storage, 77

DSP (digital signal processor), 81

dyes used in medical imaging, 18

E

edge pixels, 58

electron guns and beams, 38, 39

embossing of digital images, 75, 99, 102–103

entities, in computer-aided design, 14, 15

error values in color representations, 42, 43

escape-time fractals, 153, 154, 156, 157

extensions (file name) for graphic image files, 85

F

file header for .BMP files, 88

file name extensions for graphic image files, 85

filling shapes, 52, 58–59

filtering for digital image enhancement, 99

flatbed scanners, 77

flat shading, 120, 124–125

flickering, 39

flight simulators

　　described, 5–6

　　how they work, 8–9

　　Microsoft Flight Simulator, 146

　　in virtual reality, 169

Floyd-Steinberg filters for diffusion dithering, 37, 43

fonts

　　bitmapped, 61, 64–65

　　boldface or italic versions, 65

　　downloadable (soft), 64

　　outline, 61–62, 66–67

　　PostScript, 62

　　TrueType, 62

foreshortening, 115

fractal images, 3, 143, 153–154, 156–161

frames in animation techniques, 145

G

games. *See* video games

gantries in CAT scanning, 17, 20, 21

gloves in virtual reality, 169, 172, 173

Gouraud shading, 120, 126–127

graphics. *See* computer graphics; images

graphics files, bitmapped, 85–86, 88–89

H

halftoning, 37

handheld scanners, 77

hardware

    for color display, 35

    for video games, 25

    for virtual reality depictions, 169–172

headsets in virtual reality, 169, 172

hidden surface algorithms, 8

    z-buffering, 119, 122–123

hints (font alignment instructions), 66

holograms, 143

I

IFS (Iterated Function Systems) fractals, 153, 160–161

images

    advantages of digital processing, 75

    compressing files, 91–93, 94–97

    enhancement and special effects, 99–105

    fractal, 143, 153–154, 156–161

    inputting with digital cameras, 77, 78, 80–81

    inputting with scanners, 77, 78, 82–83

    photorealistic, 108

    storing as bitmapped files, 85–86, 88–89

images in three dimensions

    animating, 143, 145–151

    embossing, 75

    morphing, 143, 163–164, 166–167

    with projections, 115–117

    with ray tracing, 129–130, 132–133

    realism as goal, 108

    with solid modeling, 135–139

    surface lighting, shading and removal, 119–120, 122–127

    with surface modeling, 111–113

    virtual reality, 143, 169–170, 172–173

    wireframe, 111, 112, 119

Industrial Light & Magic (ILM), 163

information header for .BMP files, 88

interlaced and noninterlaced monitors, 39

interpreter software for drawing outline fonts, 66

inverse DCTs, 97

islands, 59

Iterated Function Systems (IFS) fractals, 153, 160–161

J

joysticks for video games, 25

JPEG (Joint Photographic Experts Group) image compression technique, 92–93, 96–97

K

Kodak Photo CD, 75, 77

L

Lanier, Jaron, 169

layering of CAD images, 14

lighting sources and effects, 15

    ray tracing, 129–130, 132–133

    shading, 119–120, 124–127

line-adjacency boundary fill algorithm, 52, 58–59

lines

    antialiasing, 69–71

    drawing with algorithms, 33, 51, 54–55

    drawing with computer-aided design, 14

lossless compression, 91

lossy compression, 91

M

magnetic resonance imaging (MRI), 17–18, 22–23

Mandelbrot set fractals, 153–154, 156–157

mask animation, 146–147, 150–151

masking, 146

mattes for morphing, 163

median-cut color quantization of color palettes, 45–46, 48–49

medical imaging

    computerized axial tomography (CAT or CT), 17, 18, 20–21

magnetic resonance imaging (MRI), 17, 18, 22–23

memory. *See also* RAM (random-access memory); speed considerations

    advantages of boundary fill techniques, 52

    advantages of color palette for conserving, 36

    disadvantages of bitmapped fonts, 61

    and storage space for bitmapped image files, 85–86, 91–92

memory-mapped video, 32

Microsoft Flight Simulator, 146

midpoint circle algorithm, 51, 56–57

midpoint line algorithm, 51, 54–55, 69

monitors, 32

    interlaced and noninterlaced, 39

monochrome devices, 35

    dithering for black-and-white renditions on, 37

morphing, 143, 163–164, 166–167

MRI (magnetic resonance imaging), 17–18, 22–23

N

noninterlaced monitors, 39

normal vectors, 124

O

orthogonal views in CAD, 15

outline fonts, 61–62, 66–67

P

Pacific Data Images (PDI), 163

page flipping for animation effects, 145

palettes. *See* color palettes

parallel projections, 115, 116

pattern dithering, 36, 41

perspective, 9

perspective projections, 115, 117

phosphors, 38

Photo CD, Kodak, 75, 77

photographic effects with digital images, 75, 108

PhotoMorph (North Coast Software), 167

photorealistic images, 108

Photoshop, Adobe, 75

pictures. *See* computer graphics; images

pilot training with flight simulators, 5–6, 8–9

pixels. *See also* dithering; images; resolution on monitor screens

    antialiasing, 69–71

    boundary fills, 52, 58–59

    described, 22, 28, 32

    edge, 58

    organizing into lines or shapes with scan conversion, 51, 54–57

    phosphors in, 38

    seed, 58

    spacing (dot pitch), 39

points (unit of measurement for fonts), 61

polygon meshes, 111

polygons

    drawing with computer-aided design, 14

    drawing with scan conversion, 55

Polyray shareware, 133

positron emission tomography (PET), 18

posterization, 40

PostScript fonts, 62

primitives in CSG solid modeling, 135

projections, 115–117

pucks in CAD, 14

Q

quantization matrix in JPEG image compression technique, 97

R

RAM (random-access memory). *See also* memory

    for PC-based video games, 25

    for storing soft (downloadable) fonts, 64

    VRAM for video buffers, 38

rasterizers for fonts, 66

ray tracing, 129–130, 132–133

reflected rays, 130, 133

reflection, 120, 129

refresh rates, 39

rendering, 15, 108

resolution on monitor screens, 32, 35

    trade-off with color quality, 36, 40–41

resonation in magnetic resonance imaging (MRI), 23

RF (radio-frequency) energy in magnetic resonance imaging (MRI), 17–18, 22, 23

RLE (run-length encoding) image compression technique, 91–92, 94–95

ROM (read-only memory) for arcade-based video games, 25

run length of pixel values in bitmapped images, 94

run-length tokens, 94

S

scan conversion
  for circles, 56–57
  described, 51
  for fonts, 66, 67
  for lines, 54–55

scan lines, 39

scanners, 77, 78, 82–83

screen swapping for animation effects, 145

SCSI (Small Computer System Interface), 80

seed pixels, 58

self-similarity of fractals, 158

shading
  flat, 120, 124–125
  Gouraud, 120, 126–127
  from lighting sources, 15

shadowing, 129

shadow masks, 39

shadow rays, 130, 132, 133

sharpening of digital images, 99, 100–101

soft fonts, 64

solid modeling, 135–139

specular reflection, 120

speed considerations. *See also* memory
  for algorithms for drawing lines or shapes, 51, 52
  for algorithms for filling shapes, 59
  of antialiasing, 71
  averaging vs. center point in median-cut color quantization, 49
  with double buffering for screen updates, 145–146
  for font creation, 67
  for image compression techniques, 96
  of outline fonts, 61
  of pattern vs. diffusion dithering, 41
  for ray tracing, 129
  of refresh rates, 39
  of VRAM, 38

spheres, 112

storage space considerations. *See also* memory
  with compression of bitmapped image files, 85–86, 91–92

surface modeling, 111–113
  with texture or bump mapping, 130

surface removal, 8, 15, 118, 122–123

Sutherland, Ivan, 3

T

Terminator 2: Judgement Day special effects, 108, 163

tesselation, 166, 167

text. *See* fonts

texture mapping, 130

three-dimensional images. *See* images in three dimensions

three-dimensional sound, 172

tomography, 17

trackballs in video games, 25

tracking device in virtual reality systems, 172, 173

transmission, 129

transmitted rays, 130, 132, 133

trees in CSG solid modeling, 135, 138

trichroic beam splitters, 78

true-color systems, 35

TrueType fonts, 62

Type Manager, Adobe, 66

V

vectors, normal, 124

video, memory-mapped, 32

video buffers, 35, 36, 38

video display terminals (VDTs), 32

video games, 25–26, 28–29, 143

viewing planes, 115

virtual reality, 143, 169–170, 172–173

VRAM (video RAM) for video buffers, 38

W

warping (morphing technique), 164

watercoloring digital images, 99, 104–105

weather patterns and escape-time fractals, 154

wireframe images, 111, 112, 119

X

X-rays in CAT scans (computerized axial tomography), 20, 21

Z

z-buffer algorithm, 119, 122–123

ATTENTION TEACHERS AND TRAINERS
Now You Can Teach From These Books!

ZD Press now offers instructors and trainers
the materials they need to use these books in their classes.

- An Instructor's Manual features flexible lessons designed for use in a
  10- or 15-week course (30-45 course hours).

- Student exercises and tests on floppy disk provide you with an
  easy way to tailor and/or duplicate tests as you need them.

- A Transparency Package contains all the graphics from the book, each
  on a single, full-color transparency.

- Spanish edition of *PC/Computing How Computers Work* will be available.

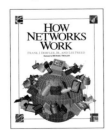

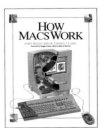

Imagination
INNOVATION·INSIGHT

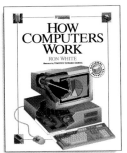

HOW COMPUTERS WORK
RON WHITE

ISBN: 094-7 Price: $22.95
Also available in Spanish.

No other books bring computer technology to life like the HOW IT WORKS series from Ziff-Davis Press. Lavish, full-color illustrations and lucid text from some of the world's top computer commentators make HOW IT WORKS books an exciting way to explore the inner workings of PC technology.

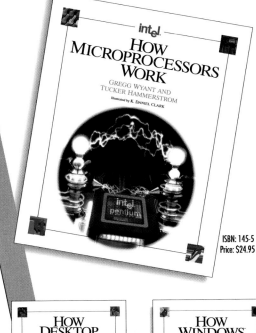

intel
HOW MICROPROCESSORS WORK
GREGG WYANT AND TUCKER HAMMERSTROM
Illustrated by K. DANIEL CLARK

ISBN: 145-5
Price: $24.95

PC Computing
HOW COMPUTERS WORK
INCLUDES INTERACTIVE CD-ROM
RON WHITE
Illustrated by T

ISBN: 250-8 Price: $39.95

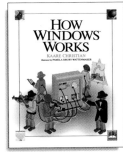

HOW DESKTOP PUBLISHING WORKS
PAMELA PFIFFNER AND BRUCE FRASER
Illustrated by DAVE FEASEY

ISBN: 191-9
Price: $24.95

HOW WINDOWS WORKS
KAARE CHRISTIAN
Illustrated by PAMELA DRURY WATTENMAKER

ISBN: 193-5 Price: $24.95

HOW COMPUTER PROGRAMMING WORKS
DANIEL APPLEMAN
Illustrated by SARAH ISHIDA

ISBN: 195-1 Price: $24.95

HOW MULTIMEDIA WORKS
ERIK HOLSINGER
Foreword by ROBERT HART and with a review from the "The Tech Top"

ISBN: 208-7 Price: $24.95

HOW THE INTERNET WORKS
JOSHUA EDDINGS
Illustrated by PAMELA DRURY WATTENMAKER

ISBN: 192-7 Price: $24.95

ZIFF-DAVIS
ZD
PRESS

Available at all fine bookstores or by calling 1-800-688-0448, ext. 100. Call for more information on the Instructor's Supplement, including transparencies for each book in the *How It Works* Series.

© 1994 Ziff-Davis Press

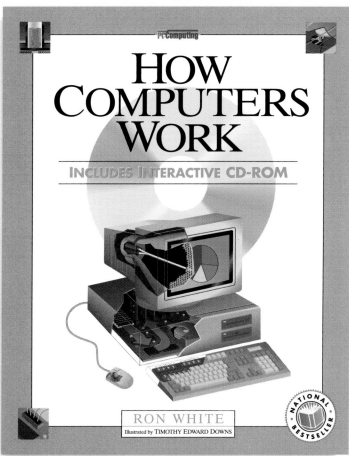

Ziff-Davis Press Survey of Readers

Please help us in our effort to produce the best books on personal computing.
For your assistance, we would be pleased to send you a FREE catalog
featuring the complete line of Ziff-Davis Press books.

1. How did you first learn about this book?

Recommended by a friend . . . . ☐ -1 (5)

Recommended by store personnel . . . . ☐ -2

Saw in Ziff-Davis Press catalog . . . . ☐ -3

Received advertisement in the mail . . . . ☐ -4

Saw the book on bookshelf at store . . . . ☐ -5

Read book review in: _____ ☐ -6

Saw an advertisement in: _____ ☐ -7

Other (Please specify): _____ ☐ -8

2. Which THREE of the following factors most influenced your decision to purchase this book? (Please check up to THREE.)

Front or back cover information on book . . . ☐ -1 (6)

Logo of magazine affiliated with book . . . . . ☐ -2

Special approach to the content . . . . ☐ -3

Completeness of content . . . . ☐ -4

Author's reputation. . . . . ☐ -5

Publisher's reputation . . . . ☐ -6

Book cover design or layout . . . . ☐ -7

Index or table of contents of book . . . . ☐ -8

Price of book . . . . ☐ -9

Special effects, graphics, illustrations . . . . . . ☐ -0

Other (Please specify): _____ ☐ -x

3. How many computer books have you purchased in the last six months? _____ (7-10)

4. On a scale of 1 to 5, where 5 is excellent, 4 is above average, 3 is average, 2 is below average, and 1 is poor, please rate each of the following aspects of this book below. (Please circle your answer.)

Depth/completeness of coverage	5	4	3	2	1	(11)
Organization of material	5	4	3	2	1	(12)
Ease of finding topic	5	4	3	2	1	(13)
Special features/time saving tips	5	4	3	2	1	(14)
Appropriate level of writing	5	4	3	2	1	(15)
Usefulness of table of contents	5	4	3	2	1	(16)
Usefulness of index	5	4	3	2	1	(17)
Usefulness of accompanying disk	5	4	3	2	1	(18)
Usefulness of illustrations/graphics	5	4	3	2	1	(19)
Cover design and attractiveness	5	4	3	2	1	(20)
Overall design and layout of book	5	4	3	2	1	(21)
Overall satisfaction with book	5	4	3	2	1	(22)

5. Which of the following computer publications do you read regularly; that is, 3 out of 4 issues?

Byte . . . . ☐ -1 (23)

Computer Shopper . . . . ☐ -2

Corporate Computing . . . . ☐ -3

Dr. Dobb's Journal . . . . ☐ -4

LAN Magazine . . . . ☐ -5

MacWEEK . . . . ☐ -6

MacUser . . . . ☐ -7

PC Computing . . . . ☐ -8

PC Magazine . . . . ☐ -9

PC WEEK . . . . ☐ -0

Windows Sources . . . . ☐ -x

Other (Please specify): _____ ☐ -y

Please turn page.

6. What is your level of experience with personal computers? With the subject of this book?

	With PCs	With subject of book
Beginner.	☐ -1 (24)	☐ -1 (25)
Intermediate.	☐ -2	☐ -2
Advanced.	☐ -3	☐ -3

7. Which of the following best describes your job title?

Officer (CEO/President/VP/owner). . . . . . . ☐ -1 (26)
Director/head. . . . . ☐ -2
Manager/supervisor. ☐ -3
Administration/staff. . . . . ☐ -4
Teacher/educator/trainer. . . . . ☐ -5
Lawyer/doctor/medical professional. . . . . . . ☐ -6
Engineer/technician. . . . . ☐ -7
Consultant. . . . . ☐ -8
Not employed/student/retired. . . . . ☐ -9
Other (Please specify): _____ ☐ -0

8. What is your age?

Under 20. . . . . ☐ -1 (27)
21-29. . . . . ☐ -2
30-39. . . . . ☐ -3
40-49. . . . . ☐ -4
50-59. . . . . ☐ -5
60 or over. . . . . ☐ -6

9. Are you:

Male. . . . . ☐ -1 (28)
Female. . . . . ☐ -2

Thank you for your assistance with this important information! Please write your address below to receive our free catalog.

Name: _____

Address: _____

City/State/Zip: _____

Fold here to mail.

2427-13-08

_____

_____

_____

BUSINESS REPLY MAIL

FIRST CLASS MAIL   PERMIT NO. 1612   OAKLAND, CA

POSTAGE WILL BE PAID BY ADDRESSEE

Ziff-Davis Press
ZIFF-DAVIS ZD PRESS
5903 Christie Avenue
Emeryville, CA 94608-1925
Attn: Marketing

NO POSTAGE
NECESSARY
IF MAILED IN
THE UNITED
STATES

Cut Here

Cut Here